W9-DDL-633

Pronounce It

PERFECTLY

in ENGLISH

SECOND EDITION

by Jean Yates, M.A.
Georgetown University

BARRON'S

BARRON'S EDUCATIONAL SERIES, INC.

Acknowledgement: The quotation from MY FAIR LADY on page 40, by permission of the Estate of Alan Jay Lerner © 1956 by Alan Jay Lerner and Frederick Loewe.

All inquiries should be addressed to:
Barron's Educational Series, Inc.
250 Wireless Boulevard
Hauppauge, NY 11788
http://www.barronseduc.com

International Standard Book No.
0-7641-2817-5 (book only),
0-7641-7749-4 (full package)

Library of Congress Catalog Card No. 2004050227

Library of Congress Cataloging-in-Publication Data
Yates, Jean.
  Pronounce it perfectly in English / by Jean Yates — 2nd ed.
    p. cm.
  ISBN 0-7641-2817-5 (book : alk. paper)—
  ISBN 0-7641-7749-4 (book/4 CDs)
    1. English language—Pronunciation—Problems,
  exercises, etc. I. Title.

PE1137.Y38 2004
428.81'3—dc22   2004050227

PRINTED IN CHINA
9 8 7 6 5 4 3 2 1

CONTENTS

PART THREE: STRESS PATTERNS

PART FOUR: INTONATION PATTERNS

PART FIVE: Appendix

Introduction

The goal of "perfect pronunciation" is not to take your personality out of your speech. Indeed, mannerisms that give hints of your origin are charming in English. The goal is, rather, to speak so that people listen to *what* you say, not *how* you say it. The goal is to be understood the first time you say something, and to be confident and proud of the way you speak.

This book and tape are designed to help you pronounce English words, phrases, and sentences correctly, so that the meaning you intend is clear and the sounds are pleasing to the ear.

The materials are organized to help you get through the maze of English spelling so that you will know how to pronounce any new word. English spelling reflects the history of the words rather than how they are pronounced. The spelling of the vowel sounds, in particular, is an unreliable guide to their pronunciation. Also, many vowel and consonant letters are silent; they are simply not pronounced at all. Most importantly, however, the pronunciation of many grammatical markers systematically changes according to the sounds that precede them, and these changes are not reflected in the spelling. Native speakers do not even notice these changes, but make them automatically. You will learn to do the same thing.

The book is divided into five parts: Vowel Sounds, Consonant Sounds, Stress Patterns, Intonation Patterns, and Appendix. Each sound is considered separately, by sound rather than by spelling. There are instructions and diagrams to show you how the sound is made. Examples are given of the sound in all possible positions in a word or phrase, and examples are given of all possible spellings of the sound. The unique stress and intonation patterns of English, which often carry meaning, are described in detail, with examples for practice. The CDs include all of these examples, modeled by native speakers, with pauses provided so that you can repeat them. The book and CDs also include exercises, quizzes, and practice materials to help you make sure you are hearing and producing the sounds correctly.

As the pronunciation of grammatical markers is vital for understanding, there are sections entitled "Usage Tips" throughout the materials. Pay particular attention to these sections. If you are a beginner, or have trouble making yourself understood, do these sections first, and continue to practice them.

Do not be discouraged if at first you do not hear the differences in sounds. You can train yourself to hear them. Follow the instructions for making the sounds; check yourself by looking in the mirror; tape-record your voice. Practice making the differences and you will begin to hear them.

The book and CDs are coordinated so that you can use them separately or together. To improve your understanding of English spelling and your recognition of written words, listen to the CDs while looking at the words and sentences in the book. When you listen to the recording without the book, simply repeat the examples during the pauses provided for writing, and do the written exercises later.

The symbols used to represent each sound are based on those of the International Phonetic Alphabet. Because many English vowel sounds are combinations of sounds, they are represented here by combinations of symbols. This is intended to help the learner form these sounds by combining their individual parts.

The pronunciation symbols used by *The American Heritage Dictionary, The Random House Dictionary, The Merriam-Webster Dictionary, The Oxford Dictionary,* and *Longman's Dictionary* appear below, so that you may use this book as a pronunciation guide for any new word you look up in your own dictionary.

Guide to Symbols

Unit	Barron's	Longman's	Oxford	Random House	American Heritage	Merriam Webster
1	ə	ə	e o i a u	ə	ə	ə
2	ɪ	ɪ	ĭ	i	ĭ	i
3	u	ʊ	o͞o	o͞o	o͞o	u̇
4	iy	iʸ	ē	e	ē	ē
5	uw	uʷ	o͞o	o͞o	o͞o	ü
6	iuw	ju	ū	yo͞o	iu	yü
7	ʌ	ʌ	ŭ	u	ŭ	'ə
8	ɛ	e	ĕ	e	ĕ	e
9	ow	əʊ	ō	ō	ō	ō
10	oiy	ɔɪ	oi	oi	oi	ȯi
11	eə	eə	ë	â	â	a
12	eiy	eɪ	ā	ā	ā	ā
13	ɔ	ɔ	aw	ô	ô	ȯ
14	æ	æ	ă	a	ă	a
15	æow	aʊ	ow	ou	ou	au̇
16	a	a	ah	ä	ŏ	ä
17	aiy	aɪ	ī	ī	ī	ī
18	p b	p b	p b	p b	p b	p b
19	t d	t d	t d	t d	t d	t d
20	k g	k g	k g	k g	k g	k g
21	f v	f v	f v	f v	f v	f v
22	ch j	ʧ ʤ	ch j	ch j	ch j	ch j
23	sh zh	ʃ ʒ	sh zh	sh zh	sh zh	sh zh
24	s z	s z	s z	s z	s z	s z
25	l r	l r	l r	l r	l r	l r
26	m n ŋ	m n ŋ	m n ng	m n ng	m n ng	m n ŋ
27	θ ð	θ ð	th dh	t̷h th	th t̷h	th <u>th</u>
28	h	h	h	h	h	h
29	w y	w j	w y	w y	w y	w y

Every vowel sound represents a syllable in a word.

Syllables are either emphasized and "stressed," or weak and "unstressed."

There are 17 different vowel sounds in English.

They all have "voice," which occurs as the vocal cords vibrate.

The tongue does not touch other parts of the mouth, teeth, or lips.

The vowel sounds differ by

- the distance between the lips
- the shape of the lips
- the length of time the sound is held

The vowel sounds are ordered in this book according to how open the mouth is. The first sound, /ə/, is made with the mouth almost closed. As the lessons progress, the mouth gradually opens. The final sound, /**aiy**/, is made with the mouth wide open.

To pronounce each vowel correctly, follow these steps:

- Look in the mirror.
- Compare your mouth with each diagram.
- Make short sounds quickly.
- Count to two, silently, for long sounds.

Unit One
The Sound /ə/

Introducing the Sound

We begin with the vowel sound /ə/ for several reasons:

- it is the most common vowel sound in English; most words of more than one syllable contain this sound in the softer, or *unstressed*, syllable,
- many one-syllable words are pronounced with this sound,
- it can be spelled with any of the five vowel letters, and also with combinations of letters,
- it is an important sound for certain grammatical markers (see pages 73, 105, 146),
- native speakers automatically know when to pronounce this sound, without being told why or in what circumstances,
- pronouncing this vowel sound correctly is one of the most important skills necessary for clear communication.

The sound /ə/ is easy to pronounce. To make it, simply open your mouth very slightly, and make a noise. It does not sound like a formed vowel, and it isn't. The lips and tongue are relaxed, and the voice makes a short, soft noise. (See Figure 1.)

/ə/ in Unstressed Syllables

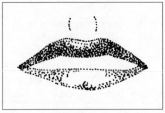

Figure 1.
The sound /ə/

3

However, it takes a lot of practice to know when to use this sound. As it can be spelled in so many different ways, we have printed in *light blue italics* the letters that are pronounced with this sound in the Examples and Exercise sections throughout this book. This will identify the sound while preserving the correct spelling of the words. When you see a vowel identified this way, pronounce it as softly and as quickly as you can, giving it no emphasis.

Listen to the following examples of words with the sound /ə/ in unstressed syllables and repeat them after the speaker.

EXAMPLES			
/ə/ in first syllable	/ə/ in second syllable		/ə/ in other syllables
a-go	so-d*a*	cap-t*ai*n	*o*-ca-si*o*n-*al*-ly
*e*f-fect	o-p*en*	pi-ge*o*n	g*a*-ra-g*e*s
*e*x-plain	den-*i*m	par-ti*a*l	poi-s*o*n-*ou*s
*o*c-cur	meth-*o*d	sta-ti*o*n	pan-*o*-ra-m*a*
u-pon	syr-*u*p	cup-bo*a*rd	u-n*i*-ver-s*al*

In addition to being spelled by all the vowel letters and combinations of letters, the /ə/ sound can also be pronounced when there is no vowel at all. Listen to the following examples, and repeat them after the speaker.

EXAMPLES	
prism	(pris-əm)
socialism	(so-c*ia*l-is-əm)
nationalism	(na-ti*o*n-*a*l-is-əm)

In certain contractions (see also pages 119, 120), the /ə/ sound is pronounced at the same time as the /n/ sound. Listen to the following examples, and repeat them after the speaker.

EXAMPLES	
doesn't	(does-ənt)
isn't	(is-ənt)
hasn't	(has-ənt)
wasn't	(was-ənt)
haven't	(hav-ənt)
didn't	(did-ənt)
hadn't	(had-ənt)
shouldn't	(should-ənt)
wouldn't	(would-ənt)
couldn't	(could-ənt)

The consonant-vowel sequence <u>le</u>, especially at the end of a word, is usually pronounced əl. Listen to the following examples, and repeat them after the speaker.

EXAMPLES	
abl*e*	(a-bəl)
cap*a*bl*e*	(cap-*a*-bəl)
suit*a*bl*e*	(suit-*a*-bəl

Usage Tip

• The words <u>a</u>, <u>an</u>, and <u>the</u> are articles, unstressed words that occur before nouns and adjective-noun combinations. Say them quickly, without emphasis. Pronounce the vowel as /ə/.

Listen to the following examples of articles containing the /ə/ sound, and repeat them after the speaker.

EXAMPLES		
a book	*a*n apple (pəl)	th*e* book
a cat	*a*n orange	th*e* cat
a dog	*a*n ice cube	th*e* dog
		th*e* un*i*verse

(When <u>the</u> occurs before a word beginning with a vowel sound, the <u>e</u> is pronounced /**iy**/. (See Unit Four, page 11.)

/ə/ in Stressed Syllables

When /ə/ is followed by the consonant /r/, it can be the prominent, or *stressed* vowel of a word. In the examples that follow, and throughout the rest of this book, the sound that is being introduced will be printed in **boldface** type.

Listen to the examples and repeat them after the speaker.

EXAMPLES		
urn	**ear**n	w**or**k
f**ur**	h**ear**d	w**or**m
p**ur**se	y**ear**ns	
		t**our**n-*a*-me nt
s**er**ve	b**ir**d	
n**er**ve	g**ir**l	syr-*u*p
	f**ir**st	

Practice for Mastery

Listen to the following sentences that feature the sound /ə/, and repeat them after the speaker.

EXAMPLES
I h**ear**d h*e*r j**our**ney w*a*s w**or**th th*e* w**or**ry.
Th*e* sug*a*r w*a*s th*e* col*o*r *o*f **ear**th.
Th*e* **ear**ly b**ir**d gets th*e* w**or**m.

Continue to practice this sound while learning the rest of the vowel sounds. Remember that the /ə/ sound will be written in *italics* when it occurs in unstressed syllables.

Introducing the Sound

To make the /ɪ/ sound, lower your jaw slightly. The lips are relaxed and are about ¼ inch (6 mm) apart. (See Figure 2.)

The sound is short.

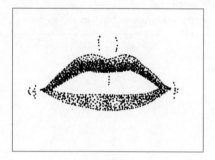

Figure 2.
The sound /ɪ/

Listen to the examples and repeat them after the speaker.

EXAMPLES			
if	gym	pretty	busy
in	symbol	English	
big			women
miss		sieve	
build			

Practice for Mastery

Listen to the following sentences featuring the vowel sound /ɪ/ and repeat them after the speaker.

EXAMPLES

Jim is in the picture.
Miss Smith is thin.
Bring chicken for dinner.
Listen to this ridiculous list.
The pretty women are busy in the gym.

Unit Three
The Sound /u/

Introducing the Sound

This vowel is formed by keeping the jaw slightly open. The lips are $\frac{1}{4}$ inch (6 mm) apart and pushed outward to make an open circle. (See Figure 3.)

The sound is short.

Figure 3.
The sound /u/

Listen to the examples and repeat them after the speaker.

EXAMPLES			
put	look	could	woman
push	book	would	wolf

Practice for Mastery

Listen to the following sentences featuring the sound /**u**/, and repeat them after the speaker.

EXAMPLES

Look in the cookbook for *a* good pudding.
He would if he could.
It should be good wool.
The woman took *a* good look *at* the wolf.

UNIT FOUR
The Sound /iy/

Introducing the Sound

To make this sound, set your lips ⅜ inch (1 cm) apart. Widen your lips into a big smile. (See Figure 4.)

The sound is long. Count to two silently to be sure it is long enough.

Figure 4.
The sound /iy/

Listen to the following examples and repeat them after the speaker.

EXAMPLES			
be	key	peopl*e*	ski
he	honey		po lice
we		*a* moeb*a*	
	cheap		suite
bee	fear	either	chassis
see		receive	de bris
sweet			
marry		niece	
happy			chamois

Usage Tips

- The <u>e</u> in the article <u>the</u> is pronounced /**iy**/ when it is followed by a word beginning with a vowel sound.

Listen to the examples and repeat them after the speaker.

EXAMPLES		
the apple	the orange	the ocean
the elephant	the onion	the umpire
the ice		

- The /**iy**/ sound, spelled <u>y</u> at the end of a word often indicates an adjective.

Listen to the examples and repeat them after the speaker.

EXAMPLES			
tricky	soapy	sticky	heavy
edgy	chilly	shaky	**ea**sy

- Adverbs often end in the syllable <u>ly</u>, pronounced /**liy**/.

Listen to the examples and repeat them after the speaker.

EXAMPLES		
nicely	quickly	slowly
plainly	sweetly	clearly

- A final /**iy**/ sound after a name can indicate endearment or informality.

Listen to the examples and repeat them after the speaker.

EXAMPLES

sweetie	Susie	daddy
Bobby	mommy	cutie

Practice for Mastery

Listen to the following sentences featuring the vowel sound /**iy**/ and repeat them after the speaker.

EXAMPLES

Jeannie, do you see the bees?
Please freeze the peas.
Neither he nor she believes me.
We can easily read the agreement.

Contrasting Sound Practice

Compare the sound /ɪ/ from Unit Two with the sound /iy/, by repeating the following words after the speaker.

EXAMPLES

/ɪ/	/iy/	/ɪ/	/iy/
bit	beet	rich	reach
sit	seat	pick	peak, peek
rip	reap	dim	deem
lip	leap	dip	deep
live	leave	sin	seen, scene
did	deed	fist	feast
hill	heel, heal, he'll	sis	cease
mill	meal	his	he's
pill	peel, peal	ship	sheep
lick	leak, leek	chip	cheap

Now listen to several sentences that feature both sounds, and repeat them after the speaker.

EXAMPLES

Six sheep were sick on the ship.
Jim eats cheap chips.
He leaves me this measly little meal.
She's as thin as he is.
Please peel the beets and string the beans.

Recognition Practice

The speaker will pronounce five words featuring these sounds. During the pauses, circle the word you hear. If it is not convenient for you to write at this time, use the pauses to repeat the words after the speaker, then complete the written exercise later. The correct answers appear below.

EXERCISE

1. sin	scene
2. live	leave
3. his	he's
4. hill	he'll
5. sit	seat

Dictation Practice

Now the speaker will pronounce five words featuring these two sounds. During the pauses, write each word on a piece of paper. If it is not convenient for you to write at this time, use the pauses to repeat the words after the speaker, then complete the written exercise later. The correct answers appear below.

Answers to Exercises

Recognition Practice, scene, live, his, he'll, seat
Dictation Practice, dip, meal, reach, sin, he's

Unit Five
The Sound /uw/

Introducing the Sound

To make the /**uw**/ sound, keep the mouth slightly open and the lips $\frac{3}{8}$ inch (1 cm) apart. The lips are tense, and pushed forward into a small circle. (See Figure 5.)

The sound is long.

Figure 5.
The sound /uw/

Listen to the examples and repeat them after the speaker.

EXAMPLES				
do	loose	flu	due	flew
lose	choose	rude	blue	new
who	food		Tuesday	
two				
canoe	through	juice	rheumatism	lieu
shoe	soup			

15

Practice for Mastery

Listen to the following sentences featuring the sound /**uw**/ and repeat them after the speaker.

EXAMPLES

Sue kn**ew** th**e** tr**u**th.
Ch**oo**se bl**u**e f**o**r th**e** n**ew** r**oo**m.
It bl**oo**ms s**oo**n, in **Ju**ne.
Th**e** n**ew**s **i**s t**oo** gl**oo**my.

Contrasting Sound Practice

Now compare the sound /**u**/ from Unit Three with the sound /**uw**/. Listen and repeat each word after the speaker.

EXAMPLES

/u/	/uw/	/u/	/uw/
f**u**ll	f**oo**l	p**u**ll	p**oo**l
st**oo**d	st**ew**ed	c**oo**kie	k**oo**ky
w**ou**ld, w**oo**d	w**oo**ed	n**oo**k	n**u**ke
h**oo**d	wh**o**'d		

Now repeat the following sentences, which feature both vowel sounds.

EXAMPLES

Lou couldn't fool Sue.
Stu wouldn't move the cooking school.
The good pool room is booked for Tuesday
    at noon.
The cook stood and looked at his new shoes.

Recognition Practice

The speaker will pronounce five words. In your book, circle the ones you hear, or repeat them now and do the written exercise later. The correct answers appear below.

Exercise

1. hood	who'd
2. full	fool
3. wood	wooed
4. nook	nuke
5. stood	stewed

Dictation Practice

Write the next five words recorded on the CD on a piece of paper, or repeat them during the pauses and write the exercise later. The correct answers appear below.

Keep in mind that learning to make the sounds correctly and practicing them will help you to hear their differences.

Spelling Challenge

Four sentences containing words with tricky spelling are next recorded on the CD. Write them down during the pauses, then check your work below. If it is not convenient for you to write at this time, repeat the sentences during the pauses, and write them later.

Answers to Exercises

Recognition Practice, hood, full, wooed, nook, stewed
Dictation Practice, who'd, stood, pool, would, full
Spelling Challenge, I see a big woman and two little women.
We drank sweet juice in the hotel suite. It's good food.
Don't shoot him in the foot.

Introducing the Sound

The /**iuw**/ sound is a combination of the sounds /**iy**/ and /**uw**/. The lips are ³⁄₈ inch (1 cm) apart. Begin with the lips spread into a big smile, then push them forward into a circle. (See Figure 6.)

The sound is short.

Figure 6.
The sound /iuw/

Listen to the examples and repeat them after the speaker.

EXAMPLES			
use	**yew**	v**ie**w	**beau**ty
cute	**few**		
m**u**sic		f**eu**d	**you**
	ewe		
			h**ue**

When /**iuw**/ occurs in unstressed syllables, the second sound of the combination changes from /**uw**/ to /**ə**/. Begin with the lips ³⁄₈ inch apart, and make the /**iy**/ sound. Move the lips to the almost-closed and relaxed position of /**ə**/.

18

Listen to the examples and repeat them after the speaker.

EXAMPLES			
figure	union	medium	accurate
failure	usually		accusation
			immunize
	canyon		
			your

Usage Tip

The article <u>a</u> is used before words that begin with a consonant sound, while <u>an</u> is used before those that begin with a vowel sound. While <u>u</u> and <u>eu</u> are vowels, when they are pronounced /**iuw**/, they actually begin with the consonant sound /**y**/ (see page 137). For this reason, use the article <u>a</u> (pronounced /ə/) instead of <u>an</u> before words beginning with /**iuw**/.

Listen to the examples, and repeat them after the speaker.

EXAMPLES
<u>u</u> pronounced as a vowel
*a*n umbrell*a*
*a*n und*e*rstanding
*a*n und*e*rstatem*e*nt
*a*n ugly situat*i*on
*a*n unusu*a*l *o*ccurr*e*nce
<u>u</u> pronounced as /**iuw**/
a uni*o*n
a use
a usef*u*l gadg*e*t
a util*i*ty
a usu*a*l *o*ccurr*e*nce

---

eu pronounced as /**iuw**/

---

a euphoric sensat*i*on
a euph*e*mism (is*ə*m)
a eul*o*gy
a Eur*o*pe*a*n

EXAMPLES

This is *a* **u**nivers*a*l truth.
It is *a* **u**niver*s*ity in New York.
They w*i*ll form *a* **un***i*on.
This *is a* **u**s**u***a*l occurrence.

Practice for Mastery

Listen to the following sentences featuring the sound /**iuw**/, and repeat them after the speaker.

EXAMPLES

A **few** b**eau**ties w*e*re in th*e* pict*u*re.
Your c**u**es *a*re conf**u**sing.
He w*a*s *a*ccused of *a*buse.
Are **you** **u**sed to **u**sing the computer?

Introducing the Sound

To make this sound, keep the mouth slightly open, with lips about ⅜ inch (1 cm) apart. (See Figure 7.)

The sound is short.

Figure 7.
The sound /ʌ/

Listen to the following examples and repeat them after the speaker.

EXAMPLES		
up	cousin	does
under	trouble (bəl)	
	rough	was
love		
done	flood	
son	blood	

Practice for Mastery

Listen to the following sentences featuring the sound /ʌ/ and repeat them after the speaker.

> **EXAMPLES**
>
> Buffy cut up the shrubs.
> The dust is under the rug.
> The mother won some of the money, but
> not enough.
> I'd love to come on Sunday if it's sunny.

Contrasting Sound Practice

To compare the /u/ from Unit Three with the sound /ʌ/, listen to the following words and repeat them after the speaker.

> **EXAMPLES**
>
> | /u/ | /ʌ/ | /u/ | /ʌ/ |
> | --- | --- | --- | --- |
> | took | tuck | put | putt |
> | look | luck | could | cud |
> | book | buck | | |

Now listen to sentences that feature both vowel sounds, and repeat them after the speaker.

> **EXAMPLES**
>
> Could you put a tuck in the front?
> Look at us for good luck.
> The bus looks good, but it's fun on foot.
> The hooded one looks tough.

Recognition Practice

Five words featuring these sounds are recorded on the CD. Circle below the words you hear. The correct answers are on page 23.

EXERCISE

1. look	luck
2. took	tuck
3. put	putt
4. could	cud
5. put	putt

Dictation Practice

Write the next five words recorded on the CD on a piece of paper, or repeat them during the pauses and write the exercise later. The correct answers appear below.

Spelling Challenge

Three sentences that have words with tricky spelling are next recorded on the CD. Listen to each one carefully, then write it down during the pause. Check your sentences below.

Answers to Exercises

Recognition Practice, luck, took, putt, could, put
Dictation Practice, luck, took, book, could, buck
Spelling Challenge, Stop rushing and pushing. The bus is busy. The poodle stood in a puddle of blood.

Introducing the Sound

To make this sound, lower your jaw slightly. The lips are tense and spread outward in a half-smile, about ½ inch (1.3 cm) apart. (See Figure 8.)

The sound is short.

Figure 8.
The sound /ɛ/

Listen to the following examples and repeat them after the speaker.

EXAMPLES			
e**gg**	*a***ga**in	m**ea**dow	fri**e**nd
edge	s**ai**d	h**ea**d	
st**e**p			h**ei**f**e**r
	s**ay**s	l**e**op*a*rd	
any			g**ue**st
m**a**ny			
c**a**n			b**u**ry

Practice for Mastery

Listen to the following sentences featuring the sound /ɛ/ and repeat them after the speaker.

24

EXAMPLES

Send Ben for his friend.
Let's rent *a* tent.
Esther never gets upset.
Fred said *it a*gain *a*nd *a*gain.

Contrasting Sound Practice

To compare the /ɪ/ sound from Unit Two with the sound /ɛ/, listen to the following words and repeat them after the speaker.

EXAMPLES

/ɪ/	/ɛ/	/ɪ/	/ɛ/
pick	peck	fill	fell
bid	bed	gym	gem
lid	led, lead	tin	ten
miss	mess	slipped	slept
wrist	rest	mitt	met
lift	left	six	sex
big	beg		

Now repeat the following sentences which feature both vowel sounds.

EXAMPLES

Pick *a* peck of pickled peppers.
Ed slipped *a*nd fell in the gym.
Evelyn missed the best bid.
Peg slept from six 'til ten, then left.

Recognition Practice

Five words featuring these sounds are recorded on the CD. Circle below the words you hear, then check them on page 27.

Exercise

1. lid	led
2. big	beg
3. slipped	slept
4. gym	gem
5. lift	left

Dictation Practice

Five words that contain these sounds are recorded on the CD. Write them during the pauses, then check them on page 27. If you have several errors, practice Units Two and Eight again.

If you do not hear the difference between the two vowel sounds, do not be discouraged. By making the sounds correctly, putting your lips and jaw in the positions described, you will begin to hear the difference.

Spelling Challenge

Three sentences containing words with tricky spelling are recorded next on the CD. During the pauses, write them down on a piece of paper. Check them on page 27.

Now compare /**iy**/ from Unit Four with the sound /ɛ/. Listen to the examples and repeat them after the speaker.

EXAMPLES

/iy/	/ɛ/	/iy/	/ɛ/
beat, beet	bet	read, reed	red, read
feel	fell	seed	said
geese	guess	sealing, ceiling	selling
he'd, heed	head	sees	says
mean	men	bleed	bled

Listen to several sentences that feature these two sounds, and repeat them after the speaker.

EXAMPLES

Please feed the pets and weed the beds.
He said he'd eat the red meat.
She says she fell and she's bleeding.
Steve guessed he'd been seen in the shed.

Recognition Practice

Five words featuring these sounds are recorded next on the CD. Circle below the ones you hear. The correct answers appear below.

EXERCISE

1. teen   ten
2. mean   men
3. heed   head
4. seal   sell
5. geese   guess

Dictation Practice

Now the speaker will pronounce five words featuring these sounds. Write the words on a piece of paper, then check your answers with the list below.

Answers to Exercises

Recognition Practice, p. 26 lid, big, slept, gem, left
Dictation Practice, p. 26 tin, miss, pick, bed, six
Spelling Challenge, The queen has been seen. He's the truest guest.
Betty is pretty already.
Recognition Practice, ten, mean, head, seal, geese
Dictation Practice, said, wrecks, feel, he'd or heed, guess

Introducing the Sound

To pronounce /**ow**/, with your lips about ½ inch (1.3 cm) apart, round them into a circle. Begin the sound, then move your lips into a smaller circle. (See Figure 9.)

The sound is long.

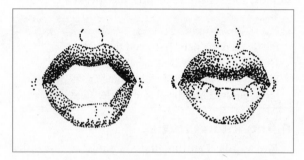

Figure 9.
The sound /ow/

Listen to the examples and repeat them after the speaker.

EXAMPLES			
ov**e**r	ye**o**man	gr**oa**n	m**au**ve
g**o**			f**au**x
zer**o**	**oh**	s**ew**	
			br**oo**ch
	dep**o**t	s**ou**l	
plat**eau**		sh**ou**lder	
	th**ough**		
owner		b**o**ne	
sl**ow**	h**oe**	st**o**ne	
wind**ow**			

28

Practice for Mastery

Listen to the following sentences featuring the sound /**ow**/ and repeat them after the speaker.

EXAMPLES

Oh n**o**, d**o**n't g**o**!
Sh**ow** J**oe** the sn**ow**m**o**bile.
Fl**o** ch**o**se t**o** r**ow** the **o**ld b**oa**t.
Thr**ow** y**ou**r st**o**le **o**ver y**ou**r sh**ou**lder.

The /**ow**/ followed by the consonant /**r**/ is slightly different. When rounding your lips, push them outward, away from the top teeth, making the /**r**/ sound. (See page 111.)

Listen to the examples and repeat them after the speaker.

EXAMPLES

or	**four**	**soar**
for	**pour**	**board**
wore		
	poor	**toward**
war	**door**	**drawer**
warm		

Practice for Mastery

Listen to the following sentences featuring the sound /**or**/, and repeat them after the speaker.

EXAMPLES

Your w**ar** st**or**ies *a*re b**or**ing.
He w**ore** sh**or**ts t**o** the st**ore**.
Pour **f**our m**ore** quarts.
M**or**ton's c**our**t rep**or**t w*a*s sh**or**t.

Contrasting Sound Practice

Now compare /ʌ/ from Unit Seven, with /ow/. Listen to the words and repeat them after the speaker.

EXAMPLES			
/ʌ/	**/ow/**	**/ʌ/**	**/ow/**
fun	phone	shun	shone
rum	roam	rub	robe
dove	dove	mud	mode, mowed
come	comb	rug	rogue
hum	home	cup	cope
crumb	chrome	nut	note

Now say the following sentences.

EXAMPLES
Bud wrote one note home.
Rose coped with the crumbs.
Lola rubbed the mud from the old rug.
Phone him at home just for fun.

Recognition Practice

The speaker will pronounce five words containing these sounds. Circle the words you hear, or repeat them now, and do the written exercise later. The answers are on page 31.

EXERCISE

1. cup	cope
2. come	comb
3. nut	note
4. fun	phone
5. shun	shone

Dictation Practice

Now write the next five words recorded on the CD on a piece of paper. Check your answers below.

Spelling Challenge

Ten sentences containing words with confusing spelling are recorded next on the tape. Write them down on a piece of paper during the pauses, then check your work below.

Answers to Exercises

Recognition Practice, p. 30 cup, comb, nut, phone, shone
Dictation Practice, p. 31 rug, note, cup, coat, home
Spelling Challenge, Whose shoes are those? Whose hose did you lose? So, sew a few new suits. Move it above the stove. Go do it. Come home. The mover put a cover over the oven. Does she have toes in her shoes? Worms have many forms. Work with the fork.

Introducing the Sound

The /**oiy**/ sound is a combination of two sounds beginning with /**o**/ and ending in /**iy**/. The lips, set about ½ inch (1.3 cm) apart, begin in a circle. (See Figure 10.) They move quickly to form a wide smile, ⅜ inch (1 cm) apart.

The sound is long.

Figure 10.
The sound /oiy/

Listen to the examples and repeat them after the speaker.

EXAMPLES		
b**oy**	b**oil**	p**oi**se
t**oy**	s**oil**	n**oi**sy
	c**oin**	

Practice for Mastery

Listen to the following sentences featuring the sound /**oiy**/, and repeat them after the speaker.

EXAMPLES

Roy's toys are noisy.
The boy pointed to the poison.
Troy's ploy was foiled.
The spoiled boy destroyed Floyd's joy.

Introducing the Sound

To make this sound, keep your jaw halfway open. The lips are ½ inch (1.3 cm) apart. Tense your lips, and form a wide, downward smile. Begin the sound, then move your lips close together into the /ə/ position. (See Figure 11.)

The sound is long.

Figure 11.
The sound /eə/

Listen to the examples and repeat them after the speaker.

Examples	
ran	laugh
fast	
pass	
craft	

To pronounce the vowel /eə/ followed by the consonant /r/, begin with the /eə/ sound, then move the lips forward into a round shape, baring the front teeth.

As before, listen to the examples and repeat them after the speaker.

EXAMPLES			
care	wear	fair	where
dare	bear	stairs	there
	aerial	heir	they're
		their	
			prayer

Practice for Mastery

Repeat the following sentences after the speaker.

EXAMPLES

The fair-haired man ran in the sand.
Where are the spare pairs Stan and Dan wear?
They're not your socks. They're theirs.
Frances laughed when she passed him on
the stairs.
They're cramming for their exams over there.

Contrasting Sound Practice

Compare /iy/, from Unit Four, with /eə/ by repeating the following words.

EXAMPLES	
/iy/	**/eə/**
leaf	laugh
mean	man
clean	clan
fiend	fanned
peace, piece	pass
leaned	land

/iy/	/eə/
we're	where, wear
beer	bear
cheer	chair
peer	pear, pair, pare
steer	stair, stare
fear	fair, fare
here, hear	hair, hare
ear	air
tear, tier	tear

Now say these sentences, which feature both vowel sounds.

EXAMPLES

Sheila ran past the stairs with a can of beer.
The lean man cheered and laughed.
She can't eat peas from a can.
We're in need of a tank of gas.

Recognition Practice

The speaker will pronounce five words. Circle the ones you hear, or repeat the words and do the written exercise later. The answers are on page 38.

EXERCISE

1. peace	pass
2. here	hair
3. we're	where
4. leaned	land
5. ear	air

Dictation Practice

Write the next five words recorded on the CD on a piece of paper, then check your work on page 38.

Contrasting Sound Practice

To compare /ɛ/ from Unit Eight with /eə/, repeat the following words after the speaker.

EXAMPLES			
/ɛ/	/eə/	/ɛ/	/eə/
lend	land	men	man
left	laughed	messed	mast
pen	pan	guess	gas
wren	ran		

Now repeat several sentences that feature these sounds.

EXAMPLES
The man laughed, then left.
I guess Ann and Ed ran out of gas.
Fran passed the pen to the man's left hand.
Can Ted send a letter to Stan?

Recognition Practice

Listen to the next five words recorded on the CD and circle the ones you hear. The answers are on page 38.

EXERCISE

1. men   man
2. pen   pan
3. wren   ran
4. lend   land
5. guess   gas

Dictation Practice

Write the next five words recorded on the CD on a piece of paper. When you finish, check your answers with the list below.

Spelling Challenge

Now write the next three sentences you hear recorded on the CD.

Check your work below.

Answers to Exercises

Recognition Practice, p. 36 pass, here, we're, land, ear
Dictation Practice, p. 37 we're, mean, steer, laugh, man
Recognition Practice, p. 37 men, pan, ran, lend, gas
Dictation Practice, laughed, guess, man, messed, pen
Spelling Challenge, There were three people here. Where were you? I can can the tomatoes.

Introducing the Sound

This is a combination of sounds. Begin with your lips in the first position of /eə/, about ½ inch (1.3 cm) apart and with a wide, downward smile. Then, slowly widen them into an upward smile, forming /iy/. (See Figure 12.)

Count to two silently to be sure the sound is long enough.

Figure 12.
The sound /eiy/

Listen to the examples and repeat them after the speaker.

EXAMPLES			
ate	cafe	prey	**eigh**t
face		they	rein
	gauge		
day		ballet	great
way	pain		
		suede	
	straight		
		fiancee	

Move your lips into the /ə/ position after /eiy/ when it occurs before the consonant /l/.

Listen to the examples and repeat them after the speaker.

EXAMPLES

pale	sail	they'll

Practice for Mastery

Repeat the following sentences which feature the sound /eiy/.

EXAMPLES

It rained eight days.
The suede cape has a great shape.
Renee ate creme brulee at the buffet today.
The rain in Spain stays mainly in the plain.
She laid the frail lace on the table.

Contrasting Sound Practice

To compare the sound /ɛ/, from Unit Eight, with /eiy/, repeat the following words.

EXAMPLES

/ɛ/	/eiy/	/ɛ/	/eiy/
red	raid	pen	pane, pain
bet	bait	wren	rain, rein, reign
debt	date	test	taste
fell	fail	shed	shade
get	gate	tent	taint
mess	mace		

Now repeat several sentences that feature both sounds.

EXAMPLES

Fred's cake failed the taste test.
Get the red dress for your date.
Jane's friend fell on the train.
Sell ten shares and trade the rest.

Recognition Practice

Five words featuring the sounds /ɛ/ and /**eiy**/ are recorded next on the CD. Circle below the words you hear, then check them below.

EXERCISE

1. pen   pain
2. test   taste
3. debt   date
4. fell   fail
5. get   gate

Dictation Practice

Five words containing these sounds are recorded next on the CD. Write them on a piece of paper during the pauses, then check them below.

Spelling Challenge

Seven sentences containing words with confusing spelling are recorded next on the CD. Listen to them carefully and write them down on a piece of paper during the pauses. Check them below.

Answers to Exercises

Recognition Practice, pain, test, debt, fail, get
Dictation Practice, red, bait, shade, fell, mess
Spelling Challenge, The pain came again. Her friend is a fiend for french fries. There were many zany women. The ape ate eight apples and an apricot. Hey, where's the key? She said she was afraid. The players said their prayers and paid their debts.

Unit Thirteen
The Sound /ɔ/

Introducing the Sound

To make the vowel sound /ɔ/, drop your jaw until the lips are $\frac{5}{8}$ inch (1.5 cm) apart. Tense your lips and round them forward halfway. (See Figure 13.)

The sound is long.

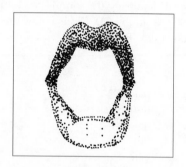

Figure 13.
The sound /ɔ/

Listen to the examples and repeat them after the speaker.

EXAMPLES			
off	all	d**augh**ter	c**ough**
on	c**all**	c**augh**t	b**ough**t
oft**e**n			
	auto	**aw**ful	br**oa**d
g**o**ne	f**au**lt	l**aw**n	

Practice for Mastery

Listen to the following sentences featuring the sound /ɔ/, and repeat them after the speaker.

42

> **EXAMPLES**
>
> Draw water from the faucet.
> The water is always calm in August.
> I thought Audrey saw a lawyer.
> You ought to have brought your daughter.

Contrasting Sound Practice

To compare /ʌ/, from Unit Seven, with /ɔ/, repeat these words after the speaker.

> **EXAMPLES**
>
> | /ʌ/ | /ɔ/ | /ʌ/ | /ɔ/ |
> |------|--------|------|--------|
> | cuff | cough | sung | song |
> | gun | gone | rung | wrong |
> | but | bought | cut | caught |
> | lung | long | gulf | golf |

Now, say the next sentences after the speaker.

> **EXAMPLES**
>
> Bud was caught with the gun he bought.
> Sunny has sung all the wrong love songs.
> Audrey bought the awesome puppies.
> Maud cut the cuffs from that awful cloth.

Recognition Practice

Listen to the next five words recorded on the CD, and circle below the ones you hear. The answers are on page 45.

1. lung	long
2. cut	caught
3. gun	gone
4. cut	caught
5. gulf	golf

Dictation Practice

Now write the next five words recorded on the CD on a piece of paper, then check your answers on page 45.

Contrasting Sound Practice

To compare /**ow**/, from Unit Nine, with /**ɔ**/, repeat the following words.

EXAMPLES

/ow/	/ɔ/	/ow/	/ɔ/
loan	lawn	loafed	loft
boat	bought	bowl	ball
coat	caught	own	on
oaf	off	boast	bossed

Now say these sentences after the speaker.

EXAMPLES

Joe caught the mole in his lawn.
Paula lost her coat on the long walk.
The tall author is his own boss.
He bought the old boat, then walked home.

Recognition Practice

Listen to the next five words recorded on the CD, and circle the ones you hear. Check your answers below.

EXERCISE

1. loafed   loft
2. coat   caught
3. bowl   ball
4. boast   bossed
5. loan   lawn

Dictation Practice

Now write the five words recorded next on the CD on a piece of paper. Check your answers below.

Spelling Challenge

Write the four sentences recorded on the tape during the pauses, then check them below.

Answers to Exercises

Recognition Practice, p. 43 lung, cut, gone, caught, golf
Dictation Practice, p. 44 song, but, gulf, cough, cuff
Recognition Practice, loafed, caught, bowl, boast, lawn
Dictation Practice, off, own, coat, bought, loaf
Spelling Challenge, The wolf plays golf. He laughed when he was caught with the faux diamond. Although the rough cough went through him, he was tough. She has gone and done it alone.

Introducing the Sound

To make this sound, keep your lips $\frac{5}{8}$ inch (1.5 cm) apart and form a half-smile, with tense lips. (See Figure 14.)

The sound is short.

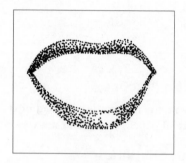

Figure 14.
The sound /æ/

Listen to the examples and repeat them after the speaker.

EXAMPLES		
back	plaid	meringue
cat		
tap		
bag		
pad		
cab		

Practice for Mastery

Listen to the following sentences featuring the sound /æ/, and repeat them after the speaker.

EXAMPLES

Pack the bags.
Have *a* snack, Jack.
Pat's cat is fat.
Her plaid jacket has black snaps.

Contrasting Sound Practice

To compare /iy/, from Unit Four, with /æ/, repeat the following words after the speaker.

EXAMPLES

/iy/	/æ/	/iy/	/æ/
feet, feat	fat	heed, he'd	had
seat	sat	he's	has
seed	sad	heat	hat
leap	lap	neat	gnat

Now repeat these sentences.

EXAMPLES

Please feed the cats.
He needs *a* black hat.
Matt has *a* shack near the sea.
She believes that Pete has had *a* nap.

Recognition Practice

Five words featuring these sounds are recorded next on the CD. Below, circle the ones you hear, then check the answers on page 49.

1. feet   fat
2. leap   lap
3. he'd   had
4. seed   sad
5. heat   hat

Dictation Practice

Write the next five words recorded on the CD on a piece of paper. When you finish, check your work on page 49.

Contrasting Sound Practice

Compare the /ɛ/ of Unit Eight with /æ/ by repeating each word after the speaker.

/ɛ/	/æ/	/ɛ/	/æ/
beg	bag	wreck	rack
head	had	set	sat
met	mat	said	sad
pet	pat	pled	plaid

Listen to the following sentences that feature /ɛ/ and /æ/, and repeat them after the speaker.

The pet cat sat on the bed.
Pat had a red rag on her head.
The men said it had a sad ending.
The next guest patted Fred on the back.

Recognition Practice

Five words featuring these sounds are recorded next on the CD. Circle them below, then check them further below.

EXERCISE

1. met   mat
2. set   sat
3. wreck   rack
4. head   had
5. said   sad

Dictation Practice

Write the next five words recorded on the CD on a piece of paper. When you finish, check your words below.

Answers to Exercises

Recognition Practice, p. 47 fat, leap, he'd, sad, heat
Dictation Practice, p. 48 sad, has, he's, seed, feet or feat
Recognition Practice, mat, set, wreck, had, sad
Dictation Practice, head, pet, said, rack, beg

Introducing the Sound

This is a combination of vowel sounds. Begin with /æ/ by setting your lips ⅝ inch (1.5 cm) apart; then, glide into /**ow**/, forming a circle with your lips. (See Figure 15.)

The sound is long.

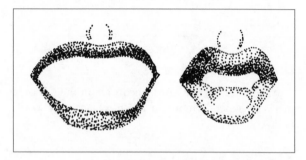

Figure 15.
The sound /æow/

Listen to the examples and repeat them after the speaker.

EXAMPLES		
h**ow**	h**ou**se	b**ough**
n**ow**	*a*l**ou**d	
br**ow**n		

To pronounce /**æow**/ before the consonant /**r**/, begin with /**æow**/, move your lips to the /ə/ position, then round them and push them outward into the /**r**/ position. This is a very long vowel sound.

Repeat the examples of the sound /**æowər**/.

50

EXAMPLES

sour   sauerkraut   power
flour
hour

Practice for Mastery

Now, repeat the following sentences featuring the sound /**æow**/.

EXAMPLES

Our townhouse has *a* brown mouse.
Are we allowed to speak aloud?
We found our gowns downtown.
Shower the flowers for *an* hour.
How's the sauerkraut?

Spelling Challenge

The next nine sentences, which contain words with tricky spelling, are recorded on the CD. Write them during the pauses, then check your work below.

Answers to Exercise

Spelling Challenge, Ouch! Don't touch me. You found out you could wound him. She wound the bandage around the wound. Slow down now. It's snowing. The rouge covered the gouge. It's my own gown. Of course the mouse couldn't eat the mousse, but my cousin could. He's the flower grower. On a tour of the mill, we bought four bags of flour.

Unit Sixteen
The Sound /a/

Introducing the Sound

To make this sound, drop your jaw until the lips are about ¾ inch (2 cm) apart, but relaxed. (See Figure 16.)

The sound is short but takes a little longer because your mouth is open so wide!

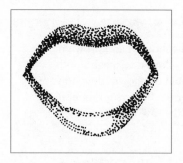

Figure 16.
The sound /a/

Listen to the examples and repeat them after the speaker.

EXAMPLES			
f**a**ther	c**o**t	**ho**nor	kn**o**wledge
w**a**nd	d**o**ll	**ho**nest	
	l**o**ck		b**u**re**au**cr**a**cy
	opti**o**n	**e**ncore	
		ennui	

Practice for Mastery

Listen to the following sentences featuring the sound /**a**/, and repeat them after the speaker.

EXAMPLES

Roz is fond of dolls.
John got an honest job.
Bob stopped in the shop for a mop.
His knowledge of crops is obvious.

Contrasting Sound Practice

Compare /ʌ/, from Unit Seven, with /a/. Repeat these words after the speaker.

EXAMPLES

/ʌ/	/a/	/ʌ/	/a/
hut	hot	shut	shot
buddy	body	putt	pot
cup	cop	gut	got
rut	rot	nut	not, knot

Now say the following sentences.

EXAMPLES

Her brother got a hot supper.
Some shots are optional.
Buddy dropped the hot cup in the shop.
Stop fussing and come up.

Recognition Practice

Five words featuring these sounds are recorded next on the CD. Circle below the ones you hear, then check them on page 55.

1. buddy	body
2. hut	hot
3. shut	shot
4. hut	hot
5. nut	not

Dictation Practice

Listen to the next five words on the CD and write them on a piece of paper during the pauses. Check them on page 55 when you finish.

The /**a**/ when followed by /**r**/, ends with the lips pushed outward; this changes the sound somewhat.

Listen to the examples and repeat them after the speaker, then listen for the confirmation.

EXAMPLES

arm	b*a*zaar	guard	serg*ea*nt
ark			
far			h*ear*t
carve			

Practice for Mastery

Listen to the following sentences, which contain the /**a**/ sound followed by /**r**/, and repeat them after the speaker.

EXAMPLES

A*r*e th*e* stars far from Mars?
Th*e* hard part is t*o* start th*e* car.
Serg*ea*nt Barton w*as* th*e* guard.
He carved a large h*ear*t in th*e* bark.

Spelling Challenge

During the pauses, write the next six sentences you hear on the CD. Check your work below.

Answers to Exercises

Recognition Practice, p. 53 body, hut, shut, hot, nut
Dictation Practice, p. 54 cop, shot, buddy, cup, knot or not
Spelling Challenge, We're here to honor the donor. Don't bother my brother or my father. They found a comb and a bomb in the tomb. Ron's son won the ribbon. Please polish the Polish medal. It's warm on the farm.

CD 2 TRACK 1

Unit Seventeen
The Sound /aiy/

Introducing the Sound

The /**aiy**/ sound is a double vowel. Begin sounding the /**a**/, with the lips about ¾ inch (2 cm) apart. Then move your lips to the /**iy**/ position, forming a big smile. (See Figure 17.)

This is a long sound.

Figure 17.
The sound /aiy/

Listen to the examples, repeat them after the speaker, then listen for the confirmation.

EXAMPLES				
I	pie	aisle	my	rye
I'd	dried		fly	
		height	guide	
ice	might		guy	indict
bike	choir	diaper	buy	

Practice for Mastery

Listen to the following sentences featuring the sound /**aiy**/, and repeat them after the speaker.

56

EXAMPLES

Id*a* b**uys** n**i**ce s**u**rpr**i**s**e**s.
I'm tw**i**ce y**ou**r s**i**ze, L**i**z*a*!
Tr**y** m**y** p**ie**, **I**r*a*!
That g**uy** m**igh**t b**uy** m**y** c**y**cl**e**.

Spelling Challenge

During the pauses, write the next three sentences
you hear on the CD, then check your work below.

Answers to Exercise

Spelling Challenge, Write down your height and weight. The police
officers are nice and polite. I find that the wind bothers my brother.

PART TWO
English Consonant Sounds

Consonant sounds are determined by
- the position of the tongue, lips, and teeth
- the way air is released
- the use of, or absence of, voice

Study Figure 18, then follow the directions for each sound.

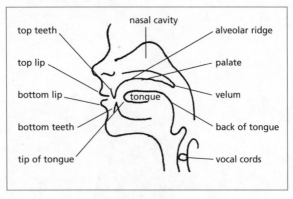

Figure 18.

Introducing the Sound /p/

To make the sound /**p**/, put your lips together firmly, stop the air completely, then pop the lips open. Do not make a vocal sound. (See Figure 19.)

At the beginning of words, release /**p**/ with a puff of air. To be sure the puff of air is strong enough, place a small piece of paper in front of your mouth when pronouncing the following words. The paper should move considerably.

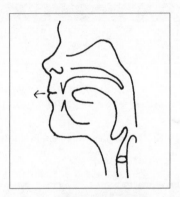

Figure 19.
The sound /p/

Listen to the following examples and repeat them after the speaker.

EXAMPLES		
pay	**p**it	**p**lay
pat	**p**ot	**p**raise
peck		

Make the same puff of air when a word ends in another consonant plus /**p**/.

61

Listen to the following examples and repeat them after the speaker.

EXAMPLES

lam**p**	har**p**	gras**p**	scal**p**
lim**p**	shar**p**	was**p**	hel**p**

Do not make the puff of air when /**p**/ occurs in the middle of a word before a vowel sound.

Listen to the following examples and repeat them after the speaker.

EXAMPLES

a**pp**le (pəl)	sim**p**le (pəl)	pur**p**le (pəl)
ha**pp**y	peo**p**le (pəl)	

Do not make the puff of air when /**p**/ directly follows the sound /**s**/ at the beginning or in the middle of a word.

Listen to the examples and repeat them after the speaker.

EXAMPLES

s**p**an	whis**p**er
s**p**end	hos**p**ital
s**p**ill	as**p**irin
s**p**oil	ex**p**ect

When /**p**/ is the last sound in a word and is followed by another word, do not pop your lips open. Bring the lips together firmly, making no vocal sound, then say the next word.

Listen to the following sentences and repeat them after the speaker.

EXAMPLES

Put the to**p** down.
Kee**p** trying.
I ho**p**e to sto**p** them.
It's u**p** there.
The ma**p** you gave me is hel**p**ful.

When /**p**/ is the last sound, make it either with or without the puff of air. There is no difference in meaning.

Listen to the following examples of sentences read both ways and repeat them after the speaker.

EXAMPLES

With the puff	**Without the puff**
Sto**p**!	Sto**p**!
Read the ma**p**.	Read the ma**p**.
Let's go on *a* tri**p**.	Let's go on *a* tri**p**.
I need some slee**p**.	I need some slee**p**.
Never give u**p**.	Never give u**p**.

Practice for Mastery

Listen to the following sentences featuring the sound /**p**/, and repeat them after the speaker.

EXAMPLES

Please **p**re**p**are the **p**izza for the **p**arty.
Pat hel**p**ed me **p**ick u**p** the **p**a**p**ers.
Put the stam**p**s on the **p**ack**a**ge.
Mr. Bisho**p** **p**aid for the lam**p** in A**p**ril.
Philli**p** didn't give me *a* map.
Penny has the hiccou**gh**s.

About the Letter p

The letter p followed by the letter h is usually pro-nounced /f/.

The letter p is silent (not pronounced) in the fol-lowing words. Listen, and repeat each word after the speaker.

EXAMPLES		
receipt	corps	cupboard
psychology	raspberry	sapphire
pneumonia		

Introducing the Sound /b/

To pronounce /b/, place your lips together firmly; stop the air completely, and make a voiced sound. (See Figure 20.)

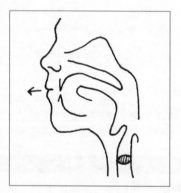

Figure 20.
The sound /b/

Listen to the following examples and repeat them after the speaker.

<blockquote>

EXAMPLES

bag	rubber
bread	sobbed
bulb	
observe	
cabs	

</blockquote>

Practice for Mastery

Listen to the following sentences featuring the sound /b/, and repeat them after the speaker.

<blockquote>

EXAMPLES

Billy grabbed the sobbing baby.

The bushes and bulbs are about to bloom.

Bob was bleeding, and his bones were broken.

Maybe Elizabeth brags a bit.

</blockquote>

About the Letter b

The letter b is silent in the following words. Listen, and repeat each word after the speaker.

<blockquote>

EXAMPLES

debt	comb	subtle
doubt	tomb	subpoena
lamb	womb	

</blockquote>

Contrasting Sound Practice

Compare the sound /p/ with the sound /b/ by repeating the following words after the speaker.

Examples

/p/	/b/
pin	**b**in
pet	**b**et
pack	**b**ack
pole	**b**owl
push	**b**ush
pour, **p**ore	**b**ore, **b**oar
punch	**b**unch
prayed	**b**raid
re**p**el	re**b**el
ra**p**id	ra**b**id
ro**p**ed	ro**b**ed
ri**pp**ed	ri**bb**ed
pare, **p**air, **p**ear	**b**are, **b**ear

Recognition Practice

Listen to the next four sentences recorded on the CD. Circle the ones you hear, or repeat the sentences now and do the written exercise later. The correct answers are below.

Exercise

1. I can't pare it.   I can't bear it.
2. Paul needs a push in   Paul needs a bush in
   front of his house.   front of his house.
3. We bought a big pole.   We bought a big bowl.
4. Patty has some   Patty has some
   new cups.   new cubs.

Answers to Exercise

Recognition Practice, I can't bear it. Paul needs a push in front of his house. We bought a big pole. Patty has some new cubs.

Introducing the Sound /t/

Place the tip of the tongue against the alveolar ridge, stop the air completely, then release the air. (See Figure 21.) Do not make a vocal sound.

There are several variations of this consonant.

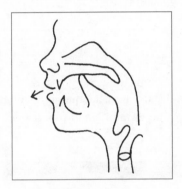

Figure 21.
The sound /t/

When a word begins with /t/, make the sound with a noisy puff of air.

To be sure the puff of air is noisy enough, hold a small piece of paper in front of your mouth when pronouncing the following words. It should move considerably.

Listen to the following examples and repeat them after the speaker.

EXAMPLES			
tame	**t**en	**t**ray	**th**yme
tap	**t**ip	**t**ree	
team		**t**win	
		twelve	

67

Make the same noisy puff when a word ends in another consonant sound plus /**t**/.

Listen to the examples and repeat them after the speaker.

EXAMPLES	
ac**t**	ap**t**
lif**t**	las**t**
faul**t**	borsch**t**
can'**t**	tex**t**

Usage Tips

• Make the same noisy puff for -**st** or -**est** at the end of an adjective to make the superlative form.

Listen to the examples and repeat them after the speaker.

EXAMPLES		
be**st**	wor**st**	mo**st**
bigg**est**	small**est**	lea**st**
happi**est**	silli**est**	

• The past tense marker, <u>ed</u>, is pronounced /**t**/, with the puff of air, when the verb ends in a voiceless consonant sound such as /**p**/, /**k**/, /**ch**/, /**f**/, /**sh**/, /**s**/, or /**ks**/. Be careful not to make a vowel sound before the /**t**/.

Listen to the examples and repeat them after the speaker.

EXAMPLES	
tap**ed**	wash**ed**
pick**ed**	pass**ed**
watch**ed**	fax**ed**
laugh**ed**	

Do not make the puff of air when /t/ follows /s/ at the beginning of a syllable.

EXAMPLES	
stamp	mistake
step	faster
stove	history

- To pronounce /t/ just before the sound /s/ at the end of words, tap the tip of your tongue on the palate, then slide your tongue forward to make /s/.

Listen to the examples and repeat them after the speaker.

EXAMPLES	
bats	cats
rests	beasts
bites	coats

To produce the /t/ at the end of words that occur before words beginning with a consonant, tap your tongue on the alveolar ridge, stop the vocal sound, then go on to the next word.

Listen to the examples and repeat them after the speaker.

EXAMPLES
She ate three hot dogs.
The fat cat sat down on the mat.
I'll bet she got the hat with that money.
I met them at the market.

In certain words, the /t/ is unreleased as above, then followed by the unstressed vowel sound /ə/, then by the sound /n/.

Listen to the examples and repeat them after the speaker.

EXAMPLES		
button	fountain	important
mitten	mountain	sentence
kitten		
bitten		

When the last word you say ends in the sound /t/, pronounce it either with or without the puff of air. There is no difference in meaning.

Listen to the following sentences read both ways, and repeat them after the speaker.

EXAMPLES	
With the puff	**Without the puff**
He sat on his hat.	He sat on his hat.
She put on her coat.	She put on her coat.
They came to visit.	They came to visit.
He didn't eat.	He didn't eat.
I didn't say that.	I didn't say that.

Practice for Mastery

Listen to the following sentences featuring the sound /t/, and repeat them after the speaker.

EXAMPLES
Those tenants tore up the apartment.
Leave the stew on the stove for two minutes.
Just a minute, please.
I put the buttons in my pocket.
Stand up straight.
Janet washed her skirt and two t-shirts.
She wished she had polished her boots.
The last time I went to that store, I got lost.

About the Letter t

The letter t, when followed by the sound /**iuw**/ is usually pronounced /**ch**/. (See Unit Twenty-two, page 90.)

When the letter t occurs between vowels, it has one of the pronunciations of the sound /**d**/. (See Introducing the Sound /**d**/, which follows.)

The letter t is silent in the following words. Listen, and repeat each word after the speaker.

EXAMPLES		
often	fasten	mortgage
listen	hasten	mustn't

See Unit Twenty-nine for the pronunciation of the letter t followed by h.

Introducing the Sound /d/

To make the sound /**d**/ place the tip of the tongue on the alveolar ridge and make a voiced sound. (See Figure 22.)

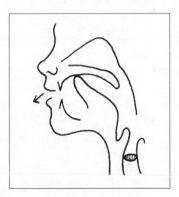

Figure 22.
The sound /d/

Hold the /**d**/ slightly at the beginning of a word, then release it with the next sound.

Listen to the examples and repeat them after the speaker.

EXAMPLES

day	**d**ress	**d**warf
dime	**d**rive	
does		
doll*a*r		
do		

At the end of words, before consonants, hold your tongue briefly on the alveolar ridge, then go on to the next word.

Listen to the examples and repeat them after the speaker.

EXAMPLES

Tell da**d** t*o* drive.
Th*e* be**d** b*e*longs t*o* me.
Th*e* li**d** fell off.
When d*o*es the ti**d**e come in?
Th*e* co**d**e number *i*s on th*e* back.

To make the sound of /**d**/ between vowels and after the consonant /**r**/, tap the tongue quickly on the palate without holding it, then go on to the next vowel.

Note that this sound is often spelled with the letters _dd_, <u>t</u>, and <u>tt</u>.

Listen to the examples and repeat them after the speaker.

EXAMPLES		
la**d**y	mu**dd**y	grate**d**
bo**d**y	a**dde**d	sub**t**l*e* (əl)
fa**d**e**d**	city	
gra**d**e**d**	la**t**er	li**tt**l*e*
har**d**er	shor**t**er	fi**tte**d
or**d**er		
da**dd**y		

Usage Tips

- To make the regular past tense, add /**d**/ to verbs that end in a vowel sound or one of the voiced consonants /**b**/, /**g**/, /**v**/, /**j**/, /**l**/, /**m**/, /**n**/, /**r**/, /**z**/, /**w**/, or /**y**/. Even though there is a letter <u>e</u> before the letter <u>d</u>, do not make a vowel sound before the /**d**/. The <u>e</u> is silent.

Listen to the examples and repeat them after the speaker.

EXAMPLES		
playe**d**	rubbe**d**	hemme**d**
staye**d**	hugge**d**	canne**d**
crie**d**	love**d**	feare**d**
snowe**d**	judge**d**	buzze**d**
glue**d**	rolle**d**	

- Add the unstressed vowel /ə/ plus /**d**/ to verbs ending with the sound /**d**/ or /**t**/. The verb now has one more syllable.

Listen to the examples and repeat them after the speaker.

EXAMPLES	
faded	wanted
ended	planted
landed	invited
folded	created
loaded	greeted

• A pronoun plus '/**d**/ forms a contraction for the modals <u>had</u> and <u>would</u>. Be careful to not use the unstressed vowel /ə/ here, which would add another syllable to the word.

Listen to the examples and repeat them after the speaker.

EXAMPLES	
I'**d** been there before.	(I had been there before.)
They'**d** called us earlier.	(They had called us earlier.)
We'**d** better stay.	(We had better stay.)
You'**d** better not do that.	(You had better not do that.)
I'**d** help you *if* I could.	(I would help you if I could.)
He'**d** come *if* he wanted to.	(He would come if he wanted to.)
We'**d** like *a* drink.	(We would like a drink.)

Practice for Mastery

Listen to the following sentences featuring the sound /**d**/, and repeat them after the speaker.

EXAMPLES

Dan **d**rove us *a*roun**d** before **d**inner.
Does **D**onn*a* have *a* **d**oll*a*r?
Davi**d** di**d**n't **d**o the **d**ishes.

He sai**d** it.
I got it.
She di**d** it.

That be**d** is ol**d**.
She ha**d** *a* ba**d** col**d**.
He ate *a* bit of butter.

Fre**d** *is a* forty-year-ol**d** veter*a*n.
Patty sat on the little la**dd**er.
E**dd**y's thirty to**d**ay.
It's *a* beau**t**i**f**ul city, b**u**t it's so dir**t**y!

About the Letter <u>d</u>

The letter <u>d</u> followed by the sound /**iuw**/ is usually pronounced /**j**/. (See Unit Twenty-two, page 90.)

The letter <u>d</u> is silent in the following words. Listen, and repeat each word after the speaker.

EXAMPLES

We**d**nesday
gran**d**father
gran**d**mother
gran**d**children
han**d**kerchief

Practice in Context

Listen to the following poem featuring the final past tense sounds /t/, /d/, and /əd/, and repeat each line after the speaker.

The Surprise Party

/**t**/

They shopped, spent, cooked, ate,
Drank, gossiped, laughed, baked,
Stopped *a*nd talked,
Worked *a*nd walked.

/**d**/

They planned, saved, sewed, schemed,
Programmed, whispered, giggled, dreamed,
Enjoyed and played,
A party made.

/**əd**/

They decorat*e*d *a*nd wait*e*d,
Then shout*e*d *a*nd celebrat*e*d.

Now listen to a tongue twister that features the sounds /t/ and /d/, and repeat each line after the speaker.

The Tutor

A tut*o*r who toot*e*d th*e* flute
Tried t*o* teach two young toot*e*rs t*o* toot,
Said th*e* two t*o* th*e* tut*o*r:
"Is it hard*e*r t*o* toot,
*o*r t*o* tut*o*r two toot*e*rs t*o* toot?"

Introducing the Sound /k/

To pronounce /**k**/, bring the back of the tongue to the velum, stop the air completely, then release it with a voiceless sound. (See Figure 23.)

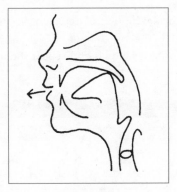

Figure 23.
The sound /k/

At the beginning of words, release /**k**/ with a puff of air. To make sure the puff of air is strong enough, hold a small piece of paper in front of your mouth as you say the following words. The paper should move considerably.

Listen to the following examples, and repeat them after the speaker.

EXAMPLES		
cat	**c**lean	**k**ettle (əl)
cost	**c**razy	
		khaki

Make the same puff of air when a word ends in another consonant plus /**k**/.

77

Listen to the following examples, and repeat them after the speaker.

EXAMPLES			
fran**k**	wor**k**	as**k**	tal**k**
in**k**	for**k**		wal**k**
		mos**q**ue	

Do not make the puff of air when /**k**/ is followed by the sound /**w**/.

Listen to the examples and repeat them after the speaker.

EXAMPLES
quick
queen
question
quite

Do not make the puff when /**k**/ occurs in the middle of a word before a vowel sound.

Listen to the following examples, and repeat them after the speaker.

EXAMPLES			
lan**k**y	sti**ck**y	un**c**le (əl)	la**cqu**er
as**k**ing	ti**ck**le (əl)	cho**c**ol**a**te	
mon**k**ey	wi**ck**ed		sa**cch**a**r**ine

When /**k**/ occurs just after the sound /**s**/, there is no puff of air.

Listen to the following examples, and repeat them after the speaker.

EXAMPLES

skin	school
skate	schedule
basket	
scrape	

When /k/ occurs just before another consonant, bring the back of the tongue to the velum, stop the air briefly, but do not release it; then make the next sound.

Listen to the examples, and repeat them after the speaker.

EXAMPLES

asks	asked	action (ak shən)
likes	liked	actor
bakes	baked	picture (pik chər)
		anxious (aŋk shəs)

Listen to the following sentences, and repeat them after the speaker.

EXAMPLES

Pick the music up tomorrow.
Look at the black bike over there.
I'll make a cake in the morning.
Did Rick rake the leaves?
Luke fell off his bike and scraped his skin.

When /k/ is the last sound in a word or sentence, pronounce it with or without the puff of air. There is no difference in meaning.

Listen to the following examples of sentences read both ways and repeat them after the speaker.

EXAMPLES	
With the puff	**Without the puff**
Don't loo**k**!	Don't loo**k**!
That's *a* fa**k**e.	That's *a* fa**k**e.
I have *a* stoma**ch** a**ch**e.	I have *a* stoma**ch** a**ch**e.

Practice for Mastery

Listen to the following sentences featuring the sound /**k**/, and repeat them after the speaker.

EXAMPLES
Can you **c**ut the **c**ake for me?
Caro**l**yn **c**ouldn't **c**ome to the **c**oncert.
His wi**ck**ed un**c**le has no s**c**ruples.
Mi**k**e *a*nd Ja**ck** **c**an work **q**ui**ck**ly.
He wal**k**s to the ban**k** every day.
They tal**k**ed *a*nd as**k**ed **q**uestions.

About the Letters k and c

The letter k is not pronounced in the following words. Listen, and repeat each word after the speaker.

EXAMPLES		
know	knowledge	knife
knew	knee	blackguard

The letter c is silent in the following word. Listen, and repeat after the speaker.

EXAMPLE
indict

Introducing the Sound /g/

To make the sound /**g**/, bring the back of the tongue to the velum, stop the air briefly, then release it with a voiced sound. (See Figure 24.)

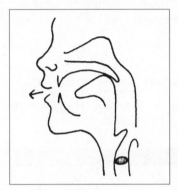

Figure 24.
The sound /g/

Listen and repeat the examples after the speaker.

EXAMPLES		
game	e**gg**	**gh**ost
glad	e**gg**s	
grade	bi**gg**er	
	ru**gg**ed	

Practice for Mastery

Listen to the following sentences featuring the sound /**g**/, and repeat them after the speaker.

> ### EXAMPLES
>
> Go get your grandmother's glasses.
> Peggy begged to go to the art gallery.
> Gloria gives gracious get-togethers.
> Please give me eight gallons of gas.
> Maggie bagged all the groceries.
> Gayle dragged the rugged luggage through
> the gate.

Contrasting Sound Practice

To compare /**g**/ with /**k**/, repeat the following words after the speaker.

EXAMPLES

/k/	/g/	/k/	/g/
cot	got	back	bag
cane	gain	pick	pig
came	game	hawk	hog
come	gum	bicker	bigger
clean	glean	sacked	sagged
curl	girl	tacked, tact	tagged
rack	rag		

Recognition Practice

The speaker will read four sentences. Circle the ones you hear, or repeat them during the pauses and do the written exercise later. The answers are on page 83.

EXERCISE

1. Gary got a clean rag.	Gary got a clean rack.
2. He is just like a hawk.	He is just like a hog.
3. We need the glue.	We need the clue.

4. Please put it in
   the back.
	Please put it in
	   the bag.

About the Letter g

The letter g after the letter n has the sound /ŋ/. See Unit Twenty-six, page 116.

The letter g is not pronounced in the following words. Listen, and repeat each word after the speaker.

EXAMPLES		
phlegm	caught, taught	weight, eight
diaphragm	bought, brought	might, light
sign	through	campaign
champagne	though	reign
lasagna	height	

Answers to Exercise

Recognition Practice, p. 82 Gary got a clean rag. He is just like a hawk. We need the glue. Please put it in the back.

Introducing the Sound /f/

To make the sound /f/, place the top teeth firmly on the inside of the bottom lip; release the air continuously with no voice. (See Figure 25.)

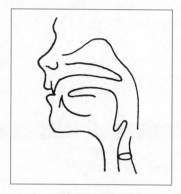

Figure 25.
The sound /f/

Listen to the examples and repeat them after the speaker.

EXAMPLES			
fall	ba**ff**le (əl)	**ph**one	lau**gh**
fish	pu**ff**ed	tro**ph**y	lau**gh**s
food	mu**ff**	Ral**ph**	lau**gh**ed
fresh		Ral**ph**'s	tou**gh**
flower	hal**f**		cou**gh**
a**f**ter		sa**pph**ire	
	o**ft**en		

Practice for Mastery

Listen to the following sentences and repeat them after the speaker.

EXAMPLES

Freddy **f**ound **f**resh **fl**owers **f**or his **f**riend.
Francie li**ft**ed her **f**inger to show o**ff** her sa**pph**ire.
Ral**ph**'s li**f**e *is* tou**gh**, but he lau**gh**s.
Phil's li**f**e *is* so**f**t, but he **f**rets.
He ate the **f**ish *a*nd ha**lf** *a* loa**f** *o*f bread, then le**ft**.

Contrasting Sound Practice

Compare the sound /**p**/, from Unit Eighteen with /**f**/ by repeating the following words after the speaker.

EXAMPLES

/p/	/f/	/p/	/f/
pin	**f**in	**p**ile	**f**ile
peel	**f**eel	**p**our	**f**our
pine	**f**ine	**p**ray	**f**ray
paid	**f**ade	**p**ride	**f**ried
pail	**f**ail	**p**ieced	**f**east
pare, **p**air, **p**ear	**f**are, **f**air	**p**up	**p**u**ff**
peer	**f**ear	si**pp**ed	si**ft**
pork	**f**ork	ri**pp**ed	ri**ft**

Recognition Practice

The speaker will read four sentences on the CD. Circle the ones you hear, or repeat them now and do the written exercise later. The answers are on page 89.

1. Please peel this fruit.	Please feel this fruit.
2. It's a pine floor.	It's a fine floor.
3. She needs the pork to make the pie.	She needs the fork to make the pie.
4. How much is the pair?	How much is the fair?

Practice in Context

Now, after the speaker, repeat each line of the following poem featuring the /**p**/ and /**f**/ sounds.

> One fresh fall day
> Paul went to the fair
> To find some fun and food.
> But while hopping a fence
> He ripped his pants,
> Which put him in a foul mood.
> But he found a fine friend
> And prayed she would mend
> The rip before it could fray;
> And although he was pieced
> With a patch on the seat
> He went to the feast anyway.

Introducing the Sound /v/

To make the sound /**v**/, place the upper teeth against the inside of the lower lip, and release the air with a voiced sound. (See Figure 26.)

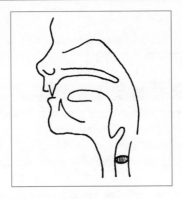

Figure 26.
The sound /v/

Listen to the following examples, repeat them after the speaker, then listen for the confirmation.

EXAMPLES		
vine	save	saves
vote	five	believes
favor	believe	saved
ever		loved
envy	of	

Usage Tip

• The contractions of <u>I have</u>, <u>you have</u>, <u>we have</u>, and <u>they have</u> are formed by adding an apostrophe ('ve) to the pronoun.

Listen to the examples and repeat them after the speaker.

EXAMPLES	
I've been there.	(I have been there.)
You've seen it.	(You have seen it.)
We've won.	(We have won.)
They've gone.	(They have gone.)

Practice for Mastery

Listen to the following sentences and repeat them after the speaker.

EXAMPLES

Evelyn arrived in evening gloves at eleven.
Val survived the five-hour drive.
She is obviously envious, and I love it.
It takes *a* lot of nerve to drive over there in the van.
They've never voted in Virginia before.

Contrasting Sound Practice

Compare the sound /b/, from Unit Eighteen with /v/. Listen to the following words, and repeat them after the speaker.

EXAMPLES

/b/	/v/	/b/	/v/
bet	vet	ballet	valet
base	vase	bent	vent
berry, bury	very	best	vest
buys	vise	marble	marvel
bail, bale	veil, vale	Serbs	serves

Recognition Practice

Four sentences are recorded on the CD. Circle the ones you hear, or repeat them during the pauses and do the written exercise later. The answers are on page 89.

When you have mastered these, try recording them on tape to compare your pronunciation with that of the speaker.

EXERCISE

1. She's a good bet.   She's a good vet.
2. We want to see   We want to see
   the ballet.   the valet.
3. I only want the best.   I only want the vest.
4. Bev's bail was stiff.   Bev's veil was stiff.

Answers to Exercises

Recognition Practice, p. 85 Please feel this fruit. It's a pine floor.
She needs the fork to make the pie. How much is the pair?
Recognition Practice, She's a good vet. We want to see the ballet.
I only want the best. Bev's veil was stiff.

Introducing the Sound /ch/

To make the sound /**ch**/, place the center of the tongue on the palate; stop the air completely, then release it abruptly with a voiceless sound. (See Figure 27.)

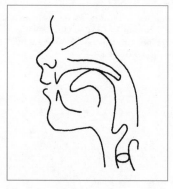

Figure 27.
The sound /ch/

Listen to the examples and repeat them after the speaker.

EXAMPLES		
chase	ca**tch**	ques**ti**on
chance	ca**tch**ing	
rea**ch**ing	ca**tch**es	
lun**ch**	wa**tch**ed	
lun**ch**es		
rea**ch**ed		

When a word or syllable beginning with the sound /**iuw**/ follows the sound /**t**/, a /**ch**/ sound is formed.

Listen to the examples and repeat them after the speaker.

EXAMPLES

situation	let you	can't you
ritual	don't you	didn't you
factual	won't you	wouldn't you
congratulations		

Practice for Mastery

Listen to the following sentences featuring the sound /**ch**/, and repeat them after the speaker.

EXAMPLES

The tea**ch**er **ch**ose **Ch**inese **Ch**eckers for the **ch**ildren.
Charles and **Ch**uck lun**ch**ed on **ch**eese and **ch**ips.
Couldn't you eat your lun**ch**, and then wat**ch** the mat**ch**?
Didn't you wat**ch** the spee**ch** on **ch**annel 7?
I can't let you ex**ch**ange the wat**ch**.

About the Letter Combination ch

The letter combination <u>ch</u> is silent in the following word. Listen and repeat.

EXAMPLE

yacht

Introducing the Sound /j/

To make the sound /**j**/, place the center of the tongue against the palate, stop the air completely, then release it abruptly with a voiced sound. (See Figure 28.)

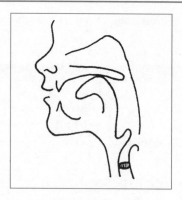

Figure 28.
The sound /j/

EXAMPLES			
jam	germ	bridge	soldier
just	gym	judged	
ajar	agency	edges	
major	region		
	huge		

The sound /**d**/ followed by /**iuw**/ is pronounced /**j**/.

Listen to the examples and repeat them after the speaker.

EXAMPLES		
education	did you	had you
graduate	would you	
individual	could you	

Practice for Mastery

Listen to the following sentences featuring the sound /j/ and then repeat them after the speaker.

EXAMPLES

I wanted you to come to my graduation.
Jim's *a* junior, majoring in education.
Would you please register at the gym?
Jill, in her jeans, jumped into her jeep.
Janice, did you see the soldier?

Introducing the Sound /sh/

To make the sound /**sh**/, touch the palate with the sides of the tongue and release the air slowly through the passageway formed down the center of the tongue. Do not stop the air flow. Do not make a sound with your voice. (See Figure 29.)

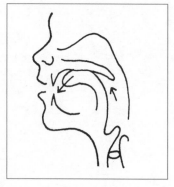

Figure 29.
The sound /sh/

Listen to the following examples and repeat them after the speaker.

EXAMPLES			
sug*a*r	**sh**ame	men**t***i*on	so**c***i*al
sure	**sh**oe		spe**c***i*al
	fa**sh***i*on	**ch**ef	
a**ss**ure	wi**sh**es	**ch**auffeur	o**ce**an
i**ss**ue	wi**sh**ed	ma**ch**ine	
an**x***iou*s	ten**s***i*on		

Practice for Mastery

Listen to the following sentences featuring the sound /**sh**/, and repeat them after the speaker.

EXAMPLES

Don't men**ti**on her an**xi**ous expre**ssi**on.
Sean a**ssu**red me he'd **sh**ine his **sh**oes.
Share the **su**g**a**r with **Ch**arlotte.
She wi**sh**ed **sh**e had gone **sh**opping.

Practice in Context

Now say this poem, one line at a time, after the speaker.

Sharon and Charlotte shopped for shallots.
The shallots were shipped from chateaux.
Sharon shared the shallots
That were shipped in the box.
Should she share the champagne, too? No!

Contrasting Sound Practice

To compare /**ch**/ from Unit Twenty-two with /**sh**/, repeat the following words after the speaker.

EXAMPLES

/ch/	/sh/	/ch/	/sh/
chin	**sh**in	**ch**eek	**ch**ic
cheese	**sh**e's	whi**ch**, wit**ch**	wi**sh**
choose	**sh**oes	wat**ch**	wa**sh**
cheap	**sh**eep	wat**ch**es	wa**sh**es
chair	**sh**are	mat**ch**ing	ma**sh**ing
chop	**sh**op	mat**ch**ed	ma**sh**ed
chip	**sh**ip	cru**tch**	cru**sh**

Recognition Practice

Four sentences are recorded on the CD. Below, circle the ones you hear, then check your work on page 97.

EXERCISE

1. Charles hurt his chin.   Charles hurt his shin.
2. This is your chair.   This is your share.
3. His witches are evil.   His wishes are evil.
4. Will you watch   Will you wash
   the baby?   the baby?

Introducing the Sound /zh/

To make the sound /**zh**/, touch your palate with the sides of your tongue, and release the air slowly through the passageway formed down the center of the tongue. Do not stop the air. Make a sound with your voice. (See Figure 30.)

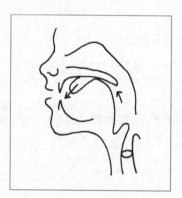

Figure 30.
The sound /zh/

Listen to the following examples and repeat them after the speaker.

EXAMPLES			
azure	measure	Asia	garage
	usual	vision	beige
		Persian	prestige
			regime
		equation	garages

This sound does not occur at the beginning of words.

Practice for Mastery

Listen to the following sentences featuring the sound /**zh**/, then repeat them after the speaker.

EXAMPLES
They usually watch television for pleasure.
She occasionally wears her beige blouse.
Take the usual measurements.
They found the treasure in Asia.

Answers to Exercise

Recognition Practice, p. 96 Charles hurt his shin. This is your chair. His wishes are evil. Will you watch the baby?

Introducing the Sound /s/

To make the sound /s/, place the center of your tongue against the palate and release the air slowly, but do not stop the air, and do not make a sound with your voice. (See Figure 31.)

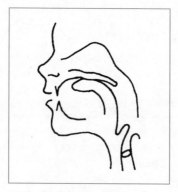

Figure 31.
The sound /s/

Listen to the following examples and repeat the words after the speaker.

EXAMPLES		
say	**sc**ene	**c**ell
some		re**c**ent
square	ki**ss**	a**c**id
small	mi**ss**ed	fa**c**e
era**s**er	bo**ss**es	
fast		walt**z**
leased	**p**sycholo**g**y	walt**z**ed

The letter <u>x</u> is often pronounced as /**k**/ + /**s**/.

98

EXAMPLES

ax	expect	fix	fox	tuxedo
relaxed	extra			
saxophone	exercise			

Be careful not to add a vowel sound before the /s/ at the beginning of a word. To avoid this, try pronouncing the /s/ at the end of the previous word.

Listen to the examples and repeat them after the speaker.

EXAMPLES

I s/peak S/panish. ("Ice peaks panish.")
Steve s/pends his pennies on s/tamps.
Scott s/kates at a s/pecial s/kating rink.
Stacy s/tays in the S/tates with her s/tepsister.

Usage Tips

- The final -s of plurals and third person (he, she, it) present tense verb forms is pronounced /s/ when it follows the voiceless consonant sounds /p/, /t/, /k/, /f/, and /θ/.
- The 's indicating possession or a contraction of <u>is</u> or <u>us</u> is also pronounced /s/ when it follows the voiceless consonants.

Listen to the following examples, repeat the words after the speaker, then listen for the confirmation.

EXAMPLES

Noun plurals	3rd-person singular verbs	Possessives and certain contractions
maps	tapes	Pat's
		Jack's
hats	hits	Ruth's
socks	cooks	
beliefs	looks	Miss Crist's
graphs	laughs	
baths		let's (let us)
wasps	grasps	it's (it is)
tests	tastes	that's (that is)
tasks	asks	what's (what is)

Practice for Mastery

Listen to the following sentences featuring the sound /s/, and repeat them after the speaker.

EXAMPLES

Let's sew some snowsuits, said Sally.
The sly fox sits in the forest and waits.
Let's ask the guests for a list of requests.
Miss Smith cooks the best feasts.
Send Sue to the store on Saturday.
Small Stephen still smiles sweetly.
Stephanie slowly spins her sled in the snow.
The Spanish speak Spanish in Spain.
It's the worst snowstorm I've seen.

About the Letter s

The letter s is silent in the following words. Listen, and repeat each word after the speaker.

EXAMPLES		
corps	chassis	chamois
aisle	debris	lisle

Contrasting Sound Practice

To compare the sound /**sh**/, from Unit Twenty-three, with /**s**/, repeat the following words.

EXAMPLES			
/sh/	**/s/**	**/sh/**	**/s/**
shoot, **ch**ute	suit	**sh**e'll	seal
shed	said	**sh**ock	sock
shower	sour	**sh**ip	sip
shoe	sue	**sh**ine	sign
show	sew, sow, so	**sh**elf	self
shame	same	**sh**ave	save
sheet	seat	lea**sh**	lease
she'd	seed	me**sh**	mess

Recognition Practice

Four sentences that feature these two sounds are recorded on the CD. Below, circle the ones you hear, then check your answers on page 108.

EXERCISE

1. It was a big shock.   It was a big sock.
2. Can you ship it?   Can you sip it?
3. Can you shave   Can you save
   my face?   my face?
4. They got good sheets.   They got good seats.

Introducing the Sound /z/

CD 2
TRACK 11

To make the /z/ sound, place the center of the tongue against the palate; release the air slowly, without stopping. Make a sound with your voice.

Figure 32.
The sound /z/

Listen to the following examples and repeat the words after the speaker.

EXAMPLES		
zero	xerox	easy
lazy	xylophone	cousin
freeze	anxiety	cheese

• The letter <u>x</u> is sometimes pronounced as /g/ + /z/.

EXAMPLES		
examine	exaggerate	exert
exact	exist	

Contrasting Sound Practice

Compare the sound /s/ with the sound /z/ by repeating the following words after the speaker.

EXAMPLES			
/s/	**/z/**	**/s/**	**/z/**
sip	zip	place	plays
Sue	zoo	cease	sees
loose	lose	raced	raised
rice	rise		

Usage Tip

• The sounds /s/ and /z/ can indicate the difference between a noun and a verb. Repeat the following examples after the speaker.

EXAMPLES	
Nouns—/s/	**Verbs—/z/**
the *a*buse	to *a*buse
the *a*dvice	to *a*dvise
the *e*xcuse	to *e*xcuse
the grease	to grease
the house	to house
the use	to use

Practice for Mastery

Now repeat these sentences after the speaker.

> *EXAMPLES*
>
> We can house five of your guests at our beach house.
> There is no use for that gadget. I can't use it.
> Victims of abuse sometimes learn to abuse others.
> When I asked him for advice, he advised me to keep quiet.
> We excused him that time, but there was no excuse for his behavior.

Usage Tips

- Noun plurals, third person present tense verb forms, possessives, and contractions after vowels and the voiced consonants /**b**/, /**d**/, /**g**/, /**v**/, /**m**/, /**n**/, /**ng**/, /**l**/, /**r**/, and /**d**/ are spelled -s or -es, and pronounced /**z**/. Be very careful *not* to pronounce the vowel e between the voiced consonant and s.

Listen to the following examples and repeat them after the speaker.

> *EXAMPLES*
>
> | Noun plurals | 3rd-person singular verbs |
> |---|---|
> | potatoes | cries |
> | labs | sees |
> | heads | does |
> | dogs | rides |
> | leaves | leaves |
> | rooms | breathes |
> | cans | comes |
> | things | runs |
> | prisms | |

Possessives	Contractions with <u>is</u>
Bob's	he's
Peg's	she's
Martha's	
his	
hers	
yours	
ours	
theirs	

Listen to the following sentences featuring the sound /z/, and repeat them after the speaker.

EXAMPLES

She's my friend's cousin.
He reads newspapers and magazines on Thursdays.
He loves his new toys.
Susan's cousin leaves on Wednesday.

• After the sounds /s/, /sh/, /z/, /zh/, /ch/ and /j/, add the unstressed vowel /ə/ before the grammatical -s. The combined sound /əz/ adds one syllable to the word.

Listen to the following examples, repeat them after the speaker, then listen for the confirmation.

EXAMPLES

Noun plurals	3rd-person singular verbs	Possessives
glasses	kisses	Bruce's
wishes	brushes	Trish's
bruises	praises	Rose's
garages	massages	Solange's
churches	matches	Mrs. Gooch's
pages	stages	Page's

Practice for Mastery

Listen to the following sentences featuring the sound /əz/ and repeat them after the speaker.

> **EXAMPLES**
>
> He washes his cars in Charles's garages.
> She teaches Bruce's niece's friend.
> Rose's daughter wishes she had new glasses.
> Mrs. Jones faxes pages of messages to our offices.
> All of Mrs. Watkins's watches are Rolexes.

Practice in Context

Listen to the following poems which feature the sounds /s/, /z/, and /əz/, and repeat them line by line during the pauses.

The Supermarket
(Plural Nouns)

What's in the store?
/s/
Carrots, beets,
Grapes, meats,
Drinks, cakes,
Soups, sweets,
Leeks, soaps,
Lots of treats.
/z/
Onions, potatoes,
Cans of tomatoes,
Breads, medicines,
Vegetables, like peas,
Non-food items,
All kinds of cheese.

/əz/

Lettuces, radishes,
Packages, juices,
Peaches, matches,
Good things for all uses,
Spices, low prices,
Some surprises,
No abuses.

The Doll
(Third-person Singular Verbs)

What does she do?
/s/
She laughs, talks,
Wets, walks,
Sleeps, drinks,
Eats, blinks,
And asks for nothing.
/z/
She soothes, cries,
Lies in the crib,
Smiles, sings,
Comfort brings.
/əz/
She dances, entrances,
Amuses, amazes,
And causes no trouble.

The Lost and Found
(Possessives and Contractions)

/s/

Whose coat is this?
It's Jack's or Rick's.
And that one?
That's either Pat's or Mick's.
This hat's pretty,
Is it Miss Smith's?
It looks like the kind
She always picks.

/z/

These shoes are big
They might be John's.
But they could be
His brother Tom's.
Who knows whose things
Are in these rooms?
Those sweaters are probably
Old Ms. Blume's.

/əz/

Galoshes, britches,
sashes, watches,
Are they Rose's,
Or Mrs. Dodge's?
They could be Charles's
Or Mrs. Welsh's,
But they're more likely
Someone else's.

Answers to Exercise

Recognition Practice, p. 101 It was a big shock. Can you sip it?
Can you save my face? They got good seats.

Introducing the Sound /l/

To pronounce /l/, curl your tongue up; put the under side of the tongue firmly on the back of your top teeth and make a sound with your voice. (See Figure 33.)

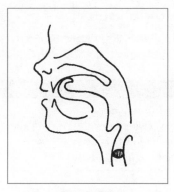

Figure 33.
The sound /l/

Listen to the examples and repeat them after the speaker.

Examples				
lake	daily	clean	male	yellow
love	solve	glass	animal	filled
	shelf	place	alcohol	will
	film			

Usage Tip

- The subject pronouns plus -'ll form contractions with the final /l/ sound of <u>will</u>, indicating some instances of future time.

109

Listen to the examples and repeat them after the speaker.

EXAMPLES

I'll	she'll	we'll
you'll	it'll (it-əl)	they'll
he'll		

Practice for Mastery

Listen to the following sentences featuring the sound /l/, and repeat them after the speaker.

EXAMPLES

Lola likes to laugh a lot.
That fellow, Luke, loves the bowling alley.
She'll like the lovely landscape.
We'll help you fill the glasses.

About the Letter l

The letter l is silent in the following words. Listen, and repeat each word after the speaker.

EXAMPLES

half	could	Lincoln
halves	should	
salve	would	

Introducing the Sound /r/

To make the sound /r/, keep the tongue back; do not let your tongue touch inside your mouth; round your lips and push them forward. Make a voiced sound. (See Figures 34A and 34B.)

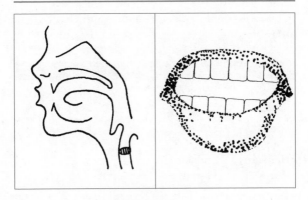

Figure 34.
The sound /r/

Listen to the examples and repeat them after the speaker.

EXAMPLES		
race	cry	around
ride	draw	carol
	from	
write	green	
	price	
	try	
	through	
mirror	pair	fears
colonel	more	fires
bird	martyr	
orphan		cared
surprise		fired

Usage Tips

• The grammar markers -s and -ed are voiced after /r/.

Listen to the following examples and repeat them after the speaker.

EXAMPLES	
/r/ + /z/	**/r/ + /d/**
fears	feared
cares	cared
fires	fired
implores	implored
lures	lured

• /r/ plus <u>e</u> is a prefix that indicates "to do again."

Listen to the examples and repeat them after the speaker.

EXAMPLES	
re-do	re-decorate
re-peat	re-write

• <u>e</u> or <u>o</u> (both pronounced /ə/) plus /r/ is a noun marker meaning "a person who does something."

Listen to the examples and repeat them after the speaker.

EXAMPLES			
teacher	sinner	actor	executor
preacher	reader	doctor	
lawyer	speeder	tutor	

• <u>e</u> plus /r/ at the end of an adjective indicates its comparative form.

Listen to the examples and repeat them after the speaker.

EXAMPLES

taller	older	shorter	younger
richer	faster	poorer	slower
sweeter	happier	dearer	sillier
nicer	friendlier	newer	cozier

• -r at the end of a pronoun can indicate possession.

Listen to the examples and repeat them after the speaker.

EXAMPLES

your	her
our	their

• 're indicates a contraction of the verb <u>are</u>.

Listen to the examples and repeat them after the speaker.

EXAMPLES

you're	they're
we're	there're

Practice for Mastery

Listen to the following sentences featuring the sound /r/ and repeat them after the speaker.

EXAMPLES

Rita read three very short stories.
Roger, the writer, brought thirty red roses.
Remember to write to your friends.
Robert ran to the store for his mother.
There're prettier flowers at the florist's.
We're here to remember our father.

Contrasting Sound Practice

To compare the sound /l/ with the sound /r/, repeat the following words after the speaker.

EXAMPLES	
/l/	**/r/**
led, lead	red, read
lift	rift
liver	river
laughed	raft
light	right, write
low	row
alive	arrive
believe	bereave
belly	berry
plays	prays, praise
climb	crime
clam	cram
flight	fright
label	labor
pale, pail	pare, pair, pear

Recognition Practice

Ten words featuring /l/ and /r/ sounds are recorded next on the CD. Below, circle the words you hear, then check your answers on page 115.

EXERCISE

1. alive	arrive		6. flight	fright
2. led	red		7. plays	prays
3. climb	crime		8. pail	pair
4. laughed	raft		9. liver	river
5. light	right		10. belly	berry

Recognition Practice

You will hear five sentences on the CD. Circle the ones you hear, then check your answers below.

EXERCISE

1. Laura prays all day.	Laura plays all day.
2. Please get me a pear.	Please get me a pail.
3. Is it right yet?	Is it light yet?
4. Can you read them?	Can you lead them?
5. The teacher corrected the tests.	The teacher collected the tests.

Practice in Context

Now repeat this poem, one line at a time, to practice /l/ and /r/.

What'll you have?

I'll have lemon pie, with lots of meringue on the top.

You'll get fat; you'll get sick; you'll be sorry tomorrow.

Never mind. I'll have diet pop.

Answers to Exercises

Recognition Practice, p. 114 arrive; red; climb; laughed; right; flight; plays; pair, pare, or pear; river; belly

Recognition Practice, Laura plays all day. Please get me a pear. Is it right yet? Can you lead them? The teacher collected the tests.

Unit Twenty-Six
The Sounds /m/,
/n/, /ŋ/

Introducing the Sound /m/

To produce the sound /m/, press your lips together and make a voiced, humming sound; release the air through your nose. (See Figure 35.)

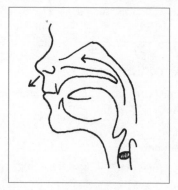

Figure 35.
The sound /m/

Listen to the following examples and repeat them after the speaker.

EXAMPLES				
maybe	to**m**orrow	na**m**e	ga**m**es	co**mb**
mother	fa**m**ous	the**m**	ta**m**ed	cli**mb**
		hi**m**	ca**m**p	
		fro**m**		

Usage Tip

- I'**m** = I am. The sound /**m**/ is the contracted verb in the sentence.

116

Practice for Mastery

Listen to the following sentences featuring the sound /m/, and repeat them after the speaker.

EXAMPLES

My na**m**e is **E**m**i**ly.
Maybe **m**y **m**other will **m**ake so**m**ething.
I'**m** co**m**ing ho**m**e with the**m** to**m**orrow.
My roo**mm**ate's fro**m** **M**aine.
I'**m** fro**m** Al**a**ba**m**a.

Introducing the Sound /n/

To pronounce /**n**/, place your tongue against your palate and hold it there; make a voiced sound and release the air through your nose. (See Figure 36.)

Figure 36.
The sound /n/

Listen to the examples and repeat them after the speaker.

EXAMPLES				
name	a**n**y	a**n**d	sane	plains
ne**v**er	mo**n**ey	a**ng**el	then	trained
		i**n**terest	e**n**vy	
know	fu**nn**y	thi**n**		

Usage Tips

- **-n** is added to the indefinite article <u>a</u> before words that begin with vowels.

The sound /**n**/ makes the difference between the articles <u>a</u> and <u>an</u>. The article <u>a</u> is used before words that begin with a consonant sound, while <u>an</u> is used before those that begin with a vowel sound. Listen to the following examples.

EXAMPLES	
Words that begin with a consonant sound	Words that begin with a vowel sound
a hat	*a*n apple
a lock	*a*n orange
a man	*a*n extra copy
a nice man	*a*n inch
a rose	*a*n elevator
a sentence	*a*n umbrella
a xerox copy	*a*n apartment

Most words that begin with the letter <u>h</u> are pronounced with the consonant sound /**h**/, and are preceded by <u>a</u>. Listen to the following examples.

EXAMPLES
a happy child
a hyster*i*cal child
a history lesson
a histor*i*c house
a histor*i*cal novel

However, the letter <u>h</u> is silent in a few words that begin with a vowel sound. <u>An</u> is used before these words. Listen to the following examples.

EXAMPLES

*a*n hon*o*r
*a*n hon*e*st answ*e*r
*a*n hon*o*r*a*ble discharge

The names for the following consonant letters actually begin with vowel sounds.

| <u>H</u> (eiych) | <u>L</u> (ɛll) | <u>M</u> (ɛm) | <u>N</u> (ɛn) |
| <u>R</u> (ar) | <u>S</u> (ɛss) | <u>X</u> (ɛks) | |

Use the article <u>an</u> when using these letters by name. Listen to the examples, and repeat them after the speaker.

EXAMPLES

*a*n HOV lane	*a*n NBC program	*a*n x-ray
*a*n LSAT test	*a*n R.S.V.P.	
*a*n MBA degree	*a*n S.O.S.	

- **-n't** is added to the verb <u>to be</u> and to auxiliary verbs to make contractions of those verbs and <u>not</u>.

When the **n't** follows the sounds /**d**/ /**t**/ /**v**/ /**s**/ /**z**/, the vowel sound /ə/ and the /**n**/ are pronounced together, adding a syllable to the word. Listen to the examples, and repeat them after the speaker.

EXAMPLES	
One syllable	Two syllables
aren't (arnt)	wouldn't (wud-ənt)
weren't (wernt)	shouldn't (shud-ənt)
don't (dont)	couldn't (cud-ənt)
can't (cant)	didn't (did-ənt)
	hadn't (had-ənt)
	mightn't (maiyt-ənt)
	haven't (have-ənt)
	isn't (is-ənt)
	hasn't (has-ənt)
	wasn't (was-ənt)
	mustn't (mus-ənt)

• -*en* is the past participle marker for many verbs.

Listen to the examples and repeat them after the speaker.

EXAMPLES		
taken	given	frozen
eaten	gotten	proven
driven		

Practice for Mastery

Listen to the following sentences featuring the sound /**n**/, and repeat them after the speaker.

EXAMPLES
The sun shines.
The thin man is an African dancer.
Mine is fine.
Tony has taken the train.
Nancy has many new friends.
They haven't eaten the tuna.

About the Letter n

The letter <u>n</u> is silent in the following words. Listen, and repeat each word after the speaker.

EXAMPLES		
aut*u*mn	col*u*mn	hymn

Contrasting Sound Practice

To compare /**m**/ with /**n**/, repeat the following words after the speaker.

EXAMPLES			
/m/	/n/	/m/	/n/
might	**n**ight	he**m**	he**n**
mere	**n**ear	la**m**e	la**n**e
di**m**e	di**n**e	si**mm**er	si**nn**er

Recognition Practice

Four sentences featuring the sounds /**m**/ and /**n**/ are recorded next on the CD. Circle the ones you hear, then check your answers on page 126.

EXERCISE

1. I'm doing the same thing.   I'm doing the sane thing

2. We would love a little sum.   We would love a little son.

3. She brought a hem for me to fix.   She brought a hen for me to fix.

4. The dimmer's on the table.   The dinner's on the table.

Introducing the Sound /ŋ/

To make the sound /ŋ/, bring the back of your tongue up against the velum, close the air off completely, and release it through the nose. (See Figure 37.)

Figure 37.
The sound /ŋ/

Listen to the examples and repeat them after the speaker.

EXAMPLES		
long	hanger	tongue
strong	singer	
singing	belonged	
going	belongings	

A double consonant sound is formed when /ng/ is followed by the sounds /g/ or /k/.

Listen to the examples and repeat them after the speaker.

EXAMPLES			
finger	stronger	thanking	sinking
longer	tangle	thinking	drinking

There are three consonant sounds together in the following words. Listen, and repeat them after the speaker.

EXAMPLES	
thanked	anxious
(ŋ + k + t)	(ŋ + k + sh)

Usage Tip

• -ing is added to the verb to form the present participle.

Listen to the examples and repeat them after the speaker.

EXAMPLES
I'm going.
She's looking.
They were shopping.
We have been looking.
The book is interesting.
The movie was fascinating.

Practice for Mastery

Listen to the following sentences featuring the sound /ŋ/ and repeat them after the speaker.

EXAMPLES
The singer sang too many long songs.
Your fingers are longer and stronger than mine.
The rings belong on the singer's finger.

Contrasting Sound Practice

Now compare the sound /**m**/ with the sound /**ŋ**/ by repeating the following words.

/m/	/ŋ/	/m/	/ŋ/
rim	ring	swimmer	swinger
rum	rung	simmer	singer
sum, some	sung	Sam	sang
swim	swing		

Dictation Practice

Listen to the four sentences recorded on the CD and write the ones you hear. Check your answers are on page 126.

EXERCISE

1. He gave me a rim last week.

   He gave me a ring last week.

2. She's dating a swimmer.

   She's dating a swinger.

3. She said she could swim it.

   She said she could swing it.

4. Mama has some good songs.

   Mama has sung good songs

Contrasting Sound Practice

Compare /**n**/ and /**ŋ**/ by repeating the following words after the speaker.

EXAMPLES			
/n/	**/ŋ/**	**/n/**	**/ŋ/**
lawn	long	stun	stung
run	rung	thin	thing
fan	fang	sin	sing

Recognition Practice

Below, circle the four sentences you hear on the CD, then check your work on page 126.

EXERCISE

1. It was a lawn party.	It was a long party.
2. It hurts him to sin.	It hurts him to sing.
3. I think she has fans.	I think she has fangs.
4. He has run four times.	He has rung four times.

Contrasting Sound Practice

Compare /m/, /n/, and /ŋ/ by repeating the following words after the speaker.

EXAMPLES		
/m/	**/n/**	**/ŋ/**
rum	run	rung
Sam	San	sang
simmer	sinner	singer
some	son, sun	sung
whim	win	wing

Practice in Context

Listen to the following dialogue featuring the sounds /**m**/, /**n**/, and /**ŋ**/, and repeat each line after the speakers.

> —Sam, how *is* your son?
> —He's fine, thanks! You know, he's nineteen now.
> —What's he doing?
> —He's going t*o* th*e* University *of* New Mexico and he's planning t*o* be *a*n eng*i*neer.
> —When *is* he coming home?
> —He's coming soon, on th*e* ninth *of* June.

Answers to Exercises

Recognition Practice, p. 121 I'm doing the sane thing. We would love a little sum. She brought a hem for me to fix. The dimmer's on the table.

Dictation Practice, p. 124 He gave me a rim last week. She's dating a swimmer. She said she could swing it. Mama has sung good songs.

Recognition Practice, p. 125 It was a lawn party. It hurts him to sing. I think she has fans. He has rung four times.

Introducing the Sound /θ/

To make the sound /θ/, hold the tip of your tongue between your top and bottom teeth; force the air out with a voiceless sound. (See Figure 38.)

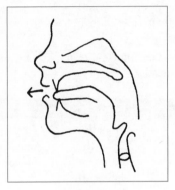

Figure 38.
The sound /θ/

Listen to the following examples and repeat them after the speaker.

EXAMPLES			
thank	tru**th**ful	heal**th**	bir**ths**
thing	weal**th**y	tee**th**	dea**ths**
thirsty	no**th**ing	mon**th**	
	some**th**ing		

Usage Tips

• -**th**, pronounced /θ/, can indicate the noun form of an adjective.

Listen to the next examples and repeat them after the speaker.

127

EXAMPLES

wid**th**	(wide)	streng**th**	(strong)
dep**th**	(deep)	bread**th**	(broad)
leng**th**	(long)		

- -**th** , pronounced /θ/, indicates all the ordinal numbers except for <u>first</u>, <u>second</u>, and <u>third</u>, and combinations that end with <u>first</u>, <u>second</u>, and <u>third</u>. It also indicates all fractions except for <u>half</u> and <u>third</u>.

Listen to the following examples and repeat them after the speaker.

EXAMPLES

four**th**	fifteen**th**	eightie**th**
fif**th**	sixteen**th**	ninetie**th**
six**th**	seventeen**th**	hundre d**th**
seven**th**	eighteen**th**	thousa n d**th**
eigh**th**	nineteen**th**	millio n**th**
nin**th**	twentie**th**	
ten**th**	thirtie**th**	one-four**th**
eleven**th**	fortie**th**	three-fif**ths**
twelf**th**	fiftie**th**	seven-eigh**ths**
thirteen**th**	sixtie**th**	
fourteen**th**	seventie**th**	

Practice for Mastery

Listen to the following sentences featuring the sound /θ/ and repeat them after the speaker.

EXAMPLES

We bo**th** need some**th**ing for our **th**roats.
He **th**ought **th**irty **th**ousa nd dolla rs wa s no**th**ing.
She took a n oa**th** to tell th e tru**th**.

Thanksgiving is on th**e** fou**r**th **Th**ursday of th**e** mon**th** of November.
Ma**th**ematics is one of her streng**th**s.
He may be weal**th**y, but he's ru**th**less and uncou**th**.

Contrasting Sound Practice

Compare the sound /s/, from Unit Twenty-four, with the sound /θ/ by repeating the following words after the speaker.

EXAMPLES

/s/	/θ/	/s/	/θ/
sin	thin	miss	myth
sing	thing	mass	math
sink	think	pass	path
sought	thought	mouse	mouth
sank	thank	force	forth, fourth
sum	thumb	truce	truth
seem, seam	theme		

Recognition Practice

Four sentences featuring the sounds /s/ and /θ/ are recorded next on the CD. Below, circle the ones you hear, then check your answers on page 132.

EXERCISE

1. The truce is
   important.
2. I sought it out.
3. He can't find
   the pass.
4. Show the teacher
   your seam.

The truth is
important.
I thought it out.
He can't find
the path.
Show the teacher
your theme.

Introducing the Sound /ð/

To pronounce /ð/, hold the tip of your tongue between your top and bottom teeth; release the air with a voiced sound. (See Figure 39.)

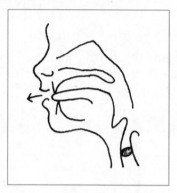

Figure 39.
The sound /ð/

Listen to the following examples and repeat them after the speaker.

EXAMPLES			
they	lather	bathe	bathes
these	together	clothe	clothes
those	breathing	breathe	soothed
the	rhythm		

Practice for Mastery

Listen to the following sentences featuring the consonant /ð/, and repeat them after the speaker.

EXAMPLES
The mother soothed the teething baby.
My brother loathes this weather.
Father seethed when he saw these leather pants.

About the Letters <u>th</u>

The letters <u>th</u> are silent in the following words. Listen, and repeat each word after the speaker.

EXAMPLES	
asth<i>m</i>a	isth<i>m</i>us

Contrasting Sound Practice

Now compare the sound /**d**/, from Unit Nineteen, with the sound /**ð**/. Repeat the words after the speaker.

EXAMPLES	
/d/	**/ð/**
dare	**th**ere, **th**eir, **th**ey're
dough	**th**ough
den	**th**en
la**dd**er	la**th**er
we**tt**er	wea**th**er, whe**th**er
le**tt**er	lea**th**er
u**tt**er, u**dd**er	o**th**er
fo**dd**er	fa**th**er
mu**tt**er	mo**th**er
writing, ri**d**ing	wri**th**ing
bree**d**	brea**th**e
sue**d**	soo**th**e
see**d**	see**th**e
skating	sca**th**ing

Recognition Practice

Listen carefully to the following four sentences on the CD, and circle below the ones you hear. Check your work on page 132.

1. Did you see the letter?	Did you see the leather?
2. He made a big ladder.	He made a big lather.
3. Yes, they sued him.	Yes, they soothe him.
4. It was his mutter that bothered her.	It was his mother that bothered her.

Answers to Exercises

Recognition Practice, p. 129 The truce is important. I sought it out. He can't find the path. Show the teacher your seam.
Recognition Practice, Did you see the letter? He made a big ladder. Yes, they soothe him. It was his mutter that bothered her.

Introducing the Sound /h/

To make the sound /**h**/, keep your tongue free and force air from the throat with a voiceless sound. (See Figure 40.)

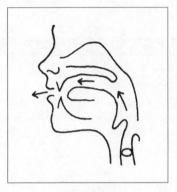

Figure 40.
The sound /h/

Listen to the examples and repeat them after the speaker.

Examples		
hay	ma**h**oga ny	w**h**o
hill	O**h**io	w**h**ole
hope	alco**h**ol	
huge	pre**h**eat	
hurry		

When the words <u>he</u>, <u>her</u>, <u>his</u>, <u>him</u>, and <u>has</u> are unstressed, the /**h**/ sound is often not pronounced.

Listen to the examples, and repeat them after the speaker.

> **EXAMPLES**
>
> I don't know where (h)e is.
> He gave it to (h)er yesterday.
> I haven't seen (h)im.

Practice for Mastery

Listen to the following sentences and repeat them after the speaker.

> **EXAMPLES**
>
> Does (h)e **h**ave any **h**ope?
> **H**i! What's y**ou**r **h**urry?
> **H**ow**a**rd is **h**iding in **Oh**io.
> They **h**ave *a* **h**uge **h**otel **a**t Lake Ta**h**oe.
> **H**er **h**usb**a**nd brought **h**ome *a* **h**uge m**a**h**oga**ny **h**utch.

About the Letter <u>h</u>

The letter <u>h</u> is silent in the following examples. Listen, and repeat each word after the speaker.

> **EXAMPLES**
>
> | | |
> |---|---|
> | hon**o**r, hon**e**st | veh**e**ment |
> | herb | exhaust |
> | heir | exhort |
> | hour | exhume |
> | | sheph**e**rd |
> | | |
> | John | what |
> | oh, ah | when |
> | night, fight, etc. | where |
> | though, through, etc. | why |
> | caught, bought, etc. | khaki |
> | | rhyth**m** |
> | | thyme |

Introducing the Sound /w/

To make the sound /**w**/, relax your tongue, then round your lips and press them back against the front of your teeth. Make a sound as you release your lips. (See Figure 41.)

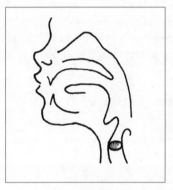

Figure 41.
The sound /w/

Listen to the examples and repeat them after the speaker.

EXAMPLES		
way	*a***w**ay	q**u**een
was		
		s**w**eet
		t**w**enty
where	*a***wh**ile	**o**ne
why		**o**nce
whistl*e* (əl)		

Practice for Mastery

Listen to the following sentences featuring the sound /w/, and repeat them after the speaker.

EXAMPLES

When will we go away?
The wind whistled in the woods.
Dwight and Duane went to Guam.
Why was there a war?
One of the twins walked twenty miles.
Wanda wore her white dress on Wednesday.
I went for a walk with Walter McGuire.

About the Letter w

The letter w is silent in the following words. Listen, and repeat each word after the speaker.

EXAMPLES

who, whom, whose, whole	two
wren, write, wrong	toward
sword	knowledge

Practice in Context

Repeat this poem after the speaker, one line at a time, to practice /w/.

Why do we have an h in *why*,
    and *where, when, what,* and *white?*
Well, there's a w in *who, whose,* and *whole,*
    and *write* when the meaning is right.

Contrasting Sound Practice

Compare the sound /v/, from Unit Twenty-one, with the sound /w/, by repeating the following words after the speaker.

EXAMPLES			
/v/	/w/	/v/	/w/
vine	wine	vow	wow
very, vary	wary	vile	while
veal	wheel, we'll	veer	we're
vent	went	vest	west
vase	ways, weighs		

Recognition Practice

Four sentences featuring the previous sounds /v/ and /w/ are recorded next on the CD. Below, circle the ones you hear, then check your answers on page 140.

EXERCISE

1. He took the veal.	He took the wheel.
2. It's in the vest.	It's in the west.
3. What's the vine like?	What's the wine like?
4. Veer to the left.	We're to the left.

Introducing the Sound /y/

To pronounce /y/, spread your tongue flat and toward the back of your mouth; do not let your tongue touch the palate. Next, make a wide smile with your lips and bring your tongue forward with a voiced sound. (See Figure 42.)

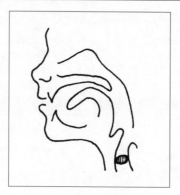

Figure 42.
The sound /y/

Listen to the following examples and repeat them after the speaker.

EXAMPLES			
yes	yet	mayor	iron (ai-yern)
yellow	year	beyond	

When the sound /**y**/ is followed by the vowel sound /**u**/, the combination is exactly the same as the vowel sound /**iuw**/.

Listen to the examples and repeat them after the speaker.

EXAMPLES				
you	youth	use	Utah	usual

Practice for Mastery

Listen to the following sentences featuring the sound /**y**/, and repeat them after the speakers.

EXAMPLES

May I use **y**o**u**r iron?
Yes, **y**ou may use it an**y** time.
He's **a** pop**u**la**r** hockey pla**y**e**r** at th**e** un**i**ve**r**sit**y**
this **y**ear.
Th**e** Miami law**y**er w**a**s triumph**a**nt **y**ester**d**ay.

About the Letter y

The letter **y** is silent in the following words. Listen,
and repeat each word after the speaker.

EXAMPLES

says   prayers

Contrasting Sound Practice

Compare the sound /**j**/ from Unit Twenty-two,
with the sound /**y**/ by repeating the following words.

EXAMPLES

/j/	/y/	/j/	/y/
jeer	**y**ear	**j**oke	**y**oke
jello	**y**ellow	**j**et	**y**et
ma**j**or	may**o**r	**g**el	**y**ell
jam	**y**am	**j**ot	**y**acht

Recognition Practice

Four sentences using the sounds /**j**/ and /**y**/ are
recorded next on the CD. Circle the ones you hear
and check your answers on page 140.

EXERCISE

1. There's no juice.	There's no use.
2. My uncle is the major.	My uncle is the mayor.
3. Has he come by jet?	Has he come by yet?
4. Are you going to jail?	Are you going to Yale?

Practice in Context

Now, repeat the following poem after the speaker, one line at a time, to practice /j/ and /y/.

> Jeremy bought *a* yellow jet,
> And then he got *a* yacht.
> "Why did you get the yacht," asked Brett,
> "When you haven't used the yellow jet yet?"

Answers to Exercises

Recognition Practice, p. 137 He took the wheel. It's in the vest. What's the wine like? We're to the left.
Recognition Practice, There's no use. My uncle is the major. Has he come by yet? Are you going to jail?

Sometimes a word ending in a consonant sound is followed by a word beginning with the same consonant sound, or one formed in the same position. To pronounce these "double consonants," do not release the sound between words. Emphasize the sound by holding it a little longer.

Listen to the following examples, and repeat them after the speaker.

EXAMPLES	
/p/ + /p/	Kee**p p**racticing
/b/ + /b/	Gra**b B**rian's hand.
/p/ + /b/	That pu**p b**elongs to her.
/t/ + /t/	It's no**t t**oo much.
/d/ + /d/	Da**d d**idn't tell me.
/t/ + /d/	Don'**t d**o that.
/k/ + /k/	I li**ke c**andy.
/g/ + /g/	That ru**g g**oes here.
/k/ + /g/	They li**ke g**reen apples.
/f/ + /f/	Keep o**ff F**reddie's flowers.
/v/ + /v/	I lo**ve V**ermont.
/v/ + /f/	He has lots **of fr**iends.
/s/ + /s/	That'**s sc**ary.
/z/ + /z/	Hi**s z**eroes are in the wrong place.
/z/ + /s/	Hi**s sc**ience class **is** interesting.
/l/ + /l/	He'**ll l**ike it.
/r/ + /r/	They **a**re **wr**ong.
/m/ + /m/	We named hi**m M**ike.
/n/ + /n/	Da**n kn**ows the truth.
/θ/ + /θ/	Are you going wi**th th**ree bags?
/θ/ + /ð/	He left wi**th the** dog.

There are two exceptions to this pattern. The sounds /ch/ and /j/ must be released before pronouncing another word.

Listen to the examples and repeat them after the speaker.

EXAMPLES	
/ch/ + /ch/	I can't reach Charles.
/j/ + /j/	Will you judge Jack's team?
/ch/ + /j/	She's going to teach geometry.

PART THREE

STRESS PATTERNS

English words can be divided into syllables. Each spoken vowel sound makes one syllable. A syllable can be

- a vowel sound alone,
- a vowel before a consonant,
- a vowel after a consonant, or
- a vowel between consonants.

Listen to these examples of one-syllable words and repeat them after the speaker.

EXAMPLES			
Vowel alone	oh	I	
Vowel-consonant	on	ice	
Consonant-vowel	to	be	you
Consonant-vowel-			
consonant	big	tough	cute

Each syllable in a word has a degree of emphasis, called stress. There are three stress levels in English, primary (**/**), secondary (/), and unstressed (–).

Each word of two or more syllables has one syllable that is longer and louder than the others. It has primary stress. In the examples that follow, these syllables are represented in **extra bold letters**.

Some words and syllables have secondary stress, which is slightly weaker than the primary one, but louder and longer than an unstressed one. These syllables are represented in **bold letters** in the examples.

There are many unstressed syllables in English. They have a short, soft vowel sound and may be difficult to hear at first. They are represented in the examples in Roman type. Unstressed vowels pronounced /ə/ are in *light blue italics*. Be careful to emphasize any consonants that occur with unstressed vowels.

Unit Thirty-Two
Two-Syllable Words

Introducing Primary Stress

A word with two vowel sounds has two syllables. One syllable has primary stress. Say it a little louder and longer than the other. Pronounce the vowel with importance.

The vowel of the unstressed syllable is usually pronounced /ə/, no matter how it is spelled. Make the vowel sound short. Pronounce the consonant sounds clearly and distinctly.

Listen to the following examples and repeat them after the speaker.

EXAMPLES			
Primary stress on first syllable		**Primary stress on second syllable**	
/	**–**	**–**	**/**
cli-	m*a*te	*ad-*	**vice**
ac-	t*o*r	*ex-*	**cite**
pleas-	*u*re	c*o*n-	**fused**
sol-	di*e*r	s*u*p-	**pose**
danc-	*e*s	s*u*r-	**prised**
wash-	*e*s		
watch-	*e*s		
fold-	*e*d		
seat-	*e*d		

The sounds /iy/, /ow/, /iuw/, and /ɪ/ often keep their normal pronunciations in unstressed syllables.

Listen to the following examples and repeat them after the speaker.

EXAMPLES

Stress on first syllable		Stress on second syllable	
l	**–**	**–**	**l**
/iy/			
ar-	my	re-	**peat**
ba-	by	de-	**duct**
ci-	ty	be-	**gin**
/ow/			
ar-	row	o-	**bey**
el-	bow	o-	**mit**
fol-	low	o-	**kay**
/iuw/			
ar-	gue	u-	**nique**
neph-	ew		
val-	ue		
/ɪ/			
build-	ing	in-	**stead**
den-	tist	in-	**sist**
mu-	sic	im-	**mune**

Usage Tip

- The stress patterns **l** – and – **l** indicate the difference between certain nouns and verbs.

Listen to the following examples and repeat them after the speaker.

EXAMPLES

Nouns		Verbs	
l	**–**	**–**	**l**
pres-	ent	pre-	**sent**
reb-	el	re-	**bel**
ob-	ject	ob-	**ject**
prog-	ress	pro-	**gress**
rec-	ord	re-	**cord**

To practice the difference in stress between nouns and verbs, repeat the following sentences after the speaker.

EXAMPLES

We're going to pre**sent** him with a **pres**ent at the reception.

His brother is a **reb**el. He re**bels** against all the established rules.

If you don't **ob**ject, I will put several **ob**jects on the table.

"When did you re**cord** your last **rec**ord?," the boy asked the singer.

Introducing Secondary Stress

CD 3
TRACK 10

Some two-syllable words have **primary** stress on the first syllable and **secondary** stress on the second syllable. Say the first syllable strongly. Emphasize the second syllable a little less, but say it with a clear vowel.

Listen to the examples and repeat them after the speaker.

EXAMPLES

/	/
ac-	cent
ath-	lete
fe-	male
in-	come
in-	sect
trans-	fer

Usage Tips

- The stress pattern **/** / is common for compound words.

Listen to the examples and repeat them after the speaker.

EXAMPLES					
Nouns		**Verbs**		**Adjectives**	
/	/	**/**	/	**/**	/
air-	plane	**dry-**	clean	**bare-**	foot
bird-	house	**black-**	mail	**care-**	free
black-	board	**brain-**	wash	**fore-**	most
drug-	store	**down-**	grade	**home-**	sick
hot-	dog	**foot-**	note	**new-**	born
land-	lord	**kid-**	nap		
make-	up				
rail-	road				

• The stress patterns **/** / and – **/** indicate the differences between some nouns and verbs.

Listen to the examples and repeat them after the speaker.

EXAMPLES			
Nouns		**Verbs**	
/	/	–	**/**
com-	bine	com-	**bine**
com-	pact	com-	**pact**
con-	duct	con-	**duct**
con-	flict	con-	**flict**
con-	tract	con-	**tract**
con-	trast	con-	**trast**
con-	vert	con-	**vert**
dis-	count	dis-	**count**
per-	mit	per-	**mit**
pro-	test	pro-	**test**
sus-	pect	sus-	**pect**

Now repeat these sentences to practice the noun-verb differences in stress.

EXAMPLES

The student's **con**duct was unacceptable.
The teacher had to conduct him to the principal.
We signed a **con**tract to buy the house.
Now we have to contract an architect to
remodel it.
The young boy's father wouldn't per**mit** him to
get a driver's **per**mit.
I sus**pect** he is one of the **sus**pects.

- The stress patterns **/** / and **/** – are important for
  distinguishing the "teen" numbers from the
  "tens." Note also that they have different pronunciations of the letter t.

Listen to the next examples and repeat them after
the speaker.

EXAMPLES

| Teens | | Tens | |
/	/	**/**	–
thir-	teen	**thir-**	ty
four-	teen	**for-**	ty
fif-	teen	**fif-**	ty
six-	teen	**six-**	ty
eigh-	teen	**eigh-**	ty
nine-	teen	**nine-**	ty

Seventeen and seventy have an additional
unstressed syllable:

| **sev** | en | **teen** | **sev** | en | ty |

Say the following poem, one line at a time, after the
speaker, to practice the tens and teens.

EXAMPLES

Have you seen my teen?
She's *a* high school queen
Between sixteen *a*nd seventeen.
She c*a*n be flirty, act like thirty,
Or *a* baby, then *a* lady,
She makes her mother feel like eighty,
Or eighteen.

• The stress patterns **/** / and **/ /** distinguish compound words from other modified nouns.

Listen to the examples that follow and repeat them after the speaker.

EXAMPLES

Compound word	Modifier + noun
/ /	**/** **/**
greenhouse	**green** **house**
bluebird	**blue** **bird**
darkroom	**dark** **room**
hotdog	**hot** **dog**
blackboard	**black** **board**

Listen to these sentences, which compare compound nouns with other modified nouns, and repeat them after the speaker.

EXAMPLES

The kitchen w*a*s *a* **dark room**.
There w*a*s *a* **dark**room in the basement for photos.
I saw *a* **blue bird** in the yard.
I don't think it w*a*s *a* **blue**bird.
They bought *a* **new house** with *a* **green**house and *a* **bird**bath in the back.

> I live in *a* **white house**, but it's not The **White**
> House.
> He said *a* few **cross words** when he couldn't
> finish the **cross**word puzzle.
> It was 100°, and Rover was one **hot dog**.
> **Hot** dogs *a*re great at baseball games.

- Some words have secondary stress on the first
  syllable, and primary on the second.

Listen to the examples and repeat them after the
speaker.

EXAMPLES			
ˌ	´	ˌ	´
car-	**toon**	un-	**do**
cash-	**ier**	un-	**pack**
Chin-	ese	up-	**date**
post-	**pone**	with-	**draw**

- Verbs with the prefix <u>re</u>, when it means "to do
  again," also have ˌ ´ as a stress pattern.

Listen to the examples and repeat them after the
speaker.

EXAMPLES					
ˌ	´	ˌ	´	ˌ	´
re-	**build**	re-	**play**	re-	**wind**
re-	**do**	re-	**set**	re-	**word**
re-	**check**	re-	**tell**	re-	**write**
re-	**heat**	re-	**think**		

- Some verbs followed by prepositions have special
  meanings, and are called <u>two-word</u> <u>verbs</u> or
  <u>phrasal</u> <u>verbs</u>. They too have the ˌ ´ stress pattern.

Listen to the examples and repeat them after the
speaker.

EXAMPLES

/	/	/	/	/	/
back	up	find	out	put	off
back	down	give	back	slow	down
back	off	give	in	take	in
call	off	give	up	take	out
calm	down	hand	in	take	off
clean	up	hand	out	use	up
dream	up	leave	out	wind	up
dress	up	put	on		

Practice for Mastery

Now repeat the following sentences featuring the / **/** stress pattern.

EXAMPLES

After we **unpack**, we'll play Chinese checkers.

I'm going to the cashier to **withdraw** the money.

She will **rewind** the **cartoon** for you.

We'll **retest** your blood and **postpone** your routine exam.

Please slow down, or we'll **wind up** on the side of the road.

Let's find out if we can **take off** next week.

I'll **call off** the next party if you don't **clean up** after this one.

Unit Thirty-Three
Words with Three
or More Syllables

Words with three or more syllables have one syllable with primary stress. The other syllables are either all unstressed, or one has secondary stress and the rest are unstressed.

Introducing Stress Pattern 1

Primary stress is on the first syllable and all other syllables are unstressed.

Listen to these examples of three-syllable words and repeat them after the speaker.

EXAMPLES					
/	–	–	**/**	–	–
a-	ni-	mal	**fin-**	ish-	es
cho-	co-	late	**vis-**	i-	ted
fur-	ni-	ture	**vis-**	i-	tor
hos-	pi-	tal	**dir-**	ti-	er
vege-	ta-	ble	**bus-**	i-	est
vis-	it-	ing	**care-**	ful-	ly
or-	ang	-es			

Listen to the following examples of four-syllable words with pattern 1, and repeat them after the speaker.

EXAMPLES							
/	–	–	–	**/**	–	–	–
for-	tu-	nate-	ly	**per-**	man-	ent-	ly
in-	no-	cent-	ly	**ser-**	i-	ous-	ly

Introducing Stress Pattern 2

Primary stress is on the second syllable and all other syllables are unstressed.

Listen to the following examples of three-syllable words and repeat them after the speaker.

EXAMPLES					
–	**/**	–	–	**/**	–
a-	**part-**	ment	ex-	**am-**	ple
ba-	**na-**	na	pro-	**hi-**	bit
con-	**di-**	tion	to-	**ge-**	ther
de-	**ci-**	sion			

Next, listen to examples of four-syllable words with pattern 2, and repeat them after the speaker.

EXAMPLES							
–	**/**	–	–	–	**/**	–	–
com-	**mu-**	ni-	ty	o-	**ri-**	gin-	al
e-	**mer-**	gen-	cy	me-	**chan-**	i-	cal
ex-	**per-**	i-	ence	se-	**cu-**	ri-	ty
in-	**fer-**	i-	or				

Following are some five-syllable words with pattern 2. Repeat them after the speaker.

EXAMPLES				
–	**/**	–	–	–
af-	**fec-**	tion-	ate-	ly
con-	**si-**	der-	a-	ble
con-	**di-**	tion-	al-	ly
co-	**op-**	er-	a-	tive
in-	**ev-**	it-	a-	ble
pro-	**fes-**	sion-	al-	ly

Introducing Stress Pattern 3

Primary stress is on the first syllable and secondary stress is on the third syllable. All other syllables are unstressed.

Listen to some examples of three-syllable words with pattern 3, and repeat them after the speaker.

Examples					
/	**–**	**/**	**/**	**–**	**/**
al-	ph*a*-	**bet**	**pho-**	to-	**graph**
bas-	ket-	**ball**	**qual-**	*i*-	**fy**
cat-	*a*-	**logue**	**re-**	cog-	**nize**
en-	ve-	**lope**	**ta-**	ble-	**cloth**
ex-	er-	**cise**	**tel-**	*e*-	**phone**
grad-	u-	**ate** (verb form)	**thun-**	der-	**storm**
hol-	*i*-	**day**			

Following are examples of four-syllable words with pattern 3. Repeat them after the speaker.

Examples							
/	_	**/**	–	**/**	_	**/**	–
dic-	tion-	**a-**	ry	**or-**	d*i*n-	**a-**	ry
com-	pl*i*-	**ca-**	ted	**tel-**	*e*-	**vi-**	s*i*on
el-	*e*-	**va-**	tor				

Introducing Stress Pattern 4

Primary stress is on the second syllable and secondary stress is on the fourth syllable. All other syllables are unstressed.

Listen to the next examples of words with pattern 4, and repeat them after the speaker.

EXAMPLES					
–	/	–	/		
a-	**pol-**	*o*-	**gize**		
*a*p-	**pre-**	ci-	ate		

EXAMPLES					
–	/	–	/		
con-	**grat-**	*u*-	**late**		
par-	**ti-**	ci-	**pate**		

Introducing Stress Pattern 5

Secondary stress is on the first syllable and primary stress is on the second syllable. The other syllables are unstressed.

Listen to the following examples of words with pattern 5 and repeat them after the speaker.

EXAMPLES					
/	/	–	/	/	–
ath-	**let-**	ic	trans-	**par-**	*e*nt
beau-	**ti-**	ci*a*n	um-	**brel-**	l*a*
out-	**stand-**	ing	va-	**ca-**	ti*o*n

Introducing Stress Pattern 6

Secondary stress is on the first syllable and primary stress is on the third syllable. All other syllables are unstressed.

Listen to the following examples of three-syllable words with pattern 6 and repeat them after the speaker.

EXAMPLES					
/	–	/	/	–	/
af-	ter-	**noon**	gas-	*o*-	**line**
dis-	*a*p-	**pear**	Jap-	*a*-	**nese**
auc-	ti*o*n-	**eer**	pi-	*o*-	**neer**
en-	gi-	**neer**	un-	der-	**stand**

Now listen to these four-syllable words that have pattern 6. Repeat them after the speaker.

Examples			
/	**–**	**/**	**–**
ad-	ver-	**tise-**	ment
ap-	pli-	**ca-**	tion
ar-	ti-	**fi-**	cial
ce-	le-	**bra-**	tion
dec-	o-	**ra-**	tion
e-	co-	**nom-**	ics
ed-	u-	**ca-**	tion
in-	de-	**pen-**	dence
man-	u-	**fac-**	ture
u-	ni-	**ver-**	sal

Prefixes are one- or two-syllable additions that occur at the beginning of some words. They carry certain meanings that modify the words.

The following examples contain one-syllable prefixes that are usually unstressed. Listen to the words and repeat them after the speaker.

EXAMPLES					
Prefix					**General meaning of prefix**
	—				
co-	co-	**op-**	*er-*	**ate**	with
con-	con-	**tin-**	ue		with
com-	com-	**mit-**	tee		with
de-	de-	**liv-**	*er*		down, from
dis-	dis-	**cuss**			negative
ex-	ex-	**hib-**	*it*		out, from
mis-	mis-	**take**			wrong
pre-	pre-	**pare**			before
pro-	pro-	**test**			for
re-	re-	**ward**			back

Other one-syllable prefixes usually have secondary stress. Listen and repeat after the speaker.

159

EXAMPLES

Prefix					General meaning of prefix
	/				
bi-	**bi-**	**o-**	lo-	gy	two
in-	**in-**	**ept**			not
ir-	**ir-**	res-	**pon-**	si- ble	not
mal-	**mal-**	**nour-**	*i*sh		badly
non-	**non-**	**poi-**	son-	*ou*s	not
pan-	**pan-**	*o-*	**ra-**	m*a*	all
post-	**post-**	**pone**			after
re-	**re-**	**write**			again
sub-	**sub-**	**let**			under
trans-	**trans-**	**fer**			across
un-	**un-**	**hap-**	py		not
vice-	**vice-**	**pres-**	*i-*	d*e*nt	deputy

As mentioned in the preceding unit, there are prefixes that have two syllables. Here are some examples:

EXAMPLES	
Prefix	**General meaning**
ante-	before
anti-	against
auto-	self
circum-	around
counter-	opposite to
hyper-	more than normal
hypo-	less than normal
inter-	between
micro-	tiny
mono-	one
multi-	many
poly-	many
uni-	one
ultra-	extreme

When these prefixes form a three-syllable word, there is usually primary stress on the first syllable, followed by an unstressed syllable and secondary stress on the third syllable.

Repeat the following examples after the speaker.

EXAMPLES					
/	**–**	**/**	**/**	**–**	**/**
an-	te-	**date**	**mi-**	cro-	**scope**
an-	ti-	**freeze**	**mon-**	o-	**rail**
au-	to-	**mat**	**mul-**	ti-	**ply**
cir-	cum-	**cize**	**u-**	ni-	**verse**
coun-	ter-	**point**	**ul-**	tra-	**sound**

161

When two-syllable prefixes form a word of four or more syllables, there is usually secondary stress on the first syllable, no stress on the second, and primary stress on the third. The remaining syllables are unstressed.

Listen carefully and repeat the next examples after the speaker.

EXAMPLES				
/	–	/	–	–
an-	te-	**ce-**	dent	
an-	ti-	**so-**	cial	
au-	to-	**ma-**	tic	
cir-	cum-	**ven-**	tion	
coun-	ter-	**clock-**	wise	
hy-	per-	**ac-**	tive	
hy-	po-	**der-**	mic	
in-	ter-	**ac-**	tion	
mi-	cro-	**sco-**	pic	
mon-	o-	**lin-**	gual	
po-	ly-	**es-**	ter	
u-	ni-	**ver-**	sal	
mul-	ti-	**na-**	tion-	al
ul-	tra-	**vi-**	o-	let

Some exceptions to this pattern are as follows. Listen, then repeat after the speaker.

EXAMPLES			
/	–	–	/
au-	to-	mo-	**bile**

/	/	–	–		/	/	–	–
an-	**ti-**	ci-	pate		mo-	**nop-**	o-	ly
an-	**ti-**	pa-	thy		mo-	**nog-**	a-	mous
an-	**tiq-**	ui-	ty		mo-	**not-**	o-	ny
an-	**tith-**	e-	sis					

Unit Thirty-Six
Suffixes

Suffixes are additions of one or more syllables that may be attached to the end of words. They usually have a grammatical function. For example, they can change the part of speech of a basic word, change the tense of a verb, and change the form of an adjective.

It is important to pronounce suffixes clearly, with the proper stress. They are almost always unstressed: Say the vowel sound quickly and with your mouth almost closed, but pronounce the consonant sounds in these syllables distinctly.

After the speaker, repeat the following words that end in unstressed one-syllable suffixes.

EXAMPLES		
Noun suffixes		
		–
-ance	im-**por-**	tance
-ant	im-**por-**	tant
-ate	**grad**-u-	ate
-ee	em-**ploy-**	ee
-ence	oc-**cur-**	rence
-ent	**cur-**	rent
-er	**driv-**	er
-ist	**so**-cial-	ist
-ment	**gov**-ern-	ment
-sion	ex-**pan-**	sion
-some	**hand-**	some
-tion	at-**ten-**	tion

EXAMPLES

Adjective suffixes

–

-al	**mu**-si-	c*a*l
-ate	**grad**-u-	*a*te
-ent	**cur-**	r*e*nt
-er	**brav-**	*e*r
-est	**brav-**	*e*st
-ful	**help-**	f*u*l
-ic	au-to-**mat-**	ic
-ive	ex-**ces-**	s*i*ve
-le	**mul**-ti-	pl*e*
-ous	**jeal-**	*ou*s

EXAMPLES

Verb suffixes

–

-ed	**want-**	*e*d
-es	**us-**	*e*s
-ing	**read-**	ing

EXAMPLES

Adverb suffixes

–   –

-ly	**slow-**	ly	**rap** *i*d	ly
			hap p*i*	ly

The following one-syllable suffixes are exceptions
to the unstressed pattern. They have secondary stress.
Repeat them after the speaker.

EXAMPLES			
Noun suffixes			
	/	–	/
-day	**hol-**	*i-*	**day**
-graph	**phot-**	*o-*	**graph**
-tude	**at-**	*ti-*	**tude**

EXAMPLES			
Verb suffixes			
	/	–	/
-ate	**grad-**	u-	**ate**
-fy	**qual-**	*i-*	**fy**
-ize	**crit-**	*i-*	**cize**

The noun suffix **-eer** has primary stress.

Repeat the next example after the speaker.

EXAMPLES					
/	–	/	/	–	/
pi-	*o-*	**neer**	**auc-**	*tio-*	**neer**
			rac-	*ke-*	**teer**

The adjective suffix **-ese** has primary stress.

Repeat the example after the speaker.

EXAMPLES					
/	–	/	/	–	/
Jap-	a-	**nese**	**Le-**	*ba-*	**nese**
			Su-	*da-*	**nese**

Some suffixes have two syllables. Both are unstressed.

Repeat the following examples after the speaker.

Examples

Noun suffixes

		–	–
-ator	**sen-**	*a-*	tor
-apher	ste-**nog-**	*ra-*	pher
-eter	ther-**mom-**	*e-*	ter
-ison	**u-**	*ni-*	son
-ity	na-ti*on*-**al-**	*i-*	ty
-ogy	bi-**o-**	lo-	gy

Examples

Adjective suffixes

		–	–
-able	**ca-**	p*a-*	ble
-ian	C*a*-**na-**	di-	*a*n
-ible	**sen-**	s*i-*	ble
-ical	**rad-**	*i-*	c*a*l
-ier	**pret-**	ti-	*e*r
-iest	**sil-**	li-	*e*st
-ior	su-**pe-**	ri-	or
-ory	**sen-**	s*o-*	ry

Examples

Adverb suffixes

		–	–
-ally	**prac-**ti-	c*a*l-	ly
-ately	**pri-**	v*a*te-	ly
-ently	**per-**m*a-*	nent-	ly
-ively	com-**pe-**ti-	tive-	ly
-ously	**ser-**i-	*ou*s-	ly

The following two examples are exceptions to the pattern. They have primary stress on the first syllable of the suffix. Listen and repeat the words after the speaker.

EXAMPLES	
	/
(noun suffix)	**for-ma-ti**o**n**
	/
(adverb suffix)	**e-vi-dent**-ly

Now repeat the following nouns that have secondary stress on the first syllable of the suffix.

EXAMPLES			
/	–	**/**	–
in-	ven-	**to-**	ry
dic-		**ta-**	tor
me-	di-	**a-**	tor
so-	cia-	**lis-**	m

Some suffixes may cause the stress of the basic word form to shift to another syllable. Repeat the examples after the speaker.

EXAMPLES	
– **/** – –	– – – **/** –
a-**pol**-o-gy	a-pol-o-**get**-ic
/ – –	– – **/** – –
cu-ri-ous	cu-ri-**os-i**-ty
– **/** – –	– – **/** –
e-**con**-o-my	ec-o-**nom**-ics
/ – –	– **/** –
i-ro-ny	i-**ron**-ic
– **/** – –	– – – **/** –
ne-**go**-ti-ate	ne-go-ti-**a-ti**o**n**

/ – /	– / – –	– / – –
pho-to-graph	pho-**tog**-ra-pher	pho-**tog**-ra-phy

/ – –	/ – / –
pol-i-tics	**pol**-i-**ti**-cian

/ –	– – / –	/ / – –
pub-lic	pub-li-**ca**-tion	**pub**-**lic**-i-ty

/ –	– / –
schol-ar	scho-**las**-tic

UNIT THIRTY-SEVEN
SENTENCE STRESS

Introducing the Patterns

When several words are spoken together in a phrase or sentence, certain words are stressed and others are spoken more softly and quickly.

Stressed Words

Four types of words are stressed in a sentence or phrase. Say them a little louder than the unstressed words. Following are examples of sentences containing only stressed words.

1. Most <u>content</u> words—nouns, verbs, adjectives, and adverbs.

Listen to the following examples of sentences formed with only content words. Repeat each sentence, imitating the speaker's stress pattern.

EXAMPLES

Charles Jones taught English.
Shirley reads aloud every day.
Aunt Janet always makes long-distance calls.
Jason plays basketball.

2. Interrogative words—<u>who</u>, <u>whose</u>, <u>when</u>, <u>where</u>, <u>why</u>, <u>what</u>, and <u>how</u>—when they begin questions.

Repeat these examples after the speaker.

EXAMPLES

Where's Mary's school?
Why's Charlie leaving?
When's Sally's party?
Who's coming?

3. Demonstrative pronouns—this, that, these, and those—when not followed by a noun.

Listen to the next examples and repeat the examples after the speaker.

EXAMPLES	
What's this?	Why are these here?
That's Jessica's ball.	We wanted those.

4. Possessive pronouns—mine, yours, his, hers, ours, theirs.

Listen to the following examples and repeat them after the speaker.

EXAMPLES	
That ticket's mine.	David sold his.
This is yours.	We bought ours yesterday.
Barbara got hers.	They gave theirs away.

Unstressed Words

There is no stress on most function words in a phrase or sentence. Here, you will find these words broken down into 13 groups. Say them quickly, but be sure to pronounce the consonants clearly. The unstressed words are printed in *italics*.

Do not stress:

1. The articles a, an, the.

Listen to your CD and repeat these examples after the speaker, trying to imitate the speaker's stress pattern.

EXAMPLES

a dog   *an* apple   *the* chair

2. Prepositions, such as <u>to</u>, <u>from</u>, <u>with</u>, <u>in</u>, <u>on</u>, <u>through</u>, <u>for</u>, <u>by</u>, <u>over</u>, <u>under</u>, etc.

Repeat the following examples after the speaker.

EXAMPLES

for a dog	*to the* hospital
with an apple	*around the* room
on the chair	*over the* hill
in the house	*after the* concert
through the door	*before the* show
of a family	

3. The subject pronouns <u>I</u>, <u>you</u>, <u>he</u>, <u>she</u>, <u>it</u>, <u>we</u>, and <u>they</u>.

Repeat these examples after the speaker.

EXAMPLES

I know *the* lesson.
You found *the* book *on the* shelf.
She tells secrets *to* everybody.
He talks *on the* phone too much.
We eat fish *on* Fridays.
They travel *to* Europe *a* lot.

4. The possessive pronouns <u>my</u>, <u>your</u>, <u>his</u>, <u>her</u>, <u>our</u>, <u>their</u>.

Repeat these examples after the speaker.

EXAMPLES

my car	*her* dress	*our* house
your friend	*his* brother	*their* camera

5. The object pronouns <u>me</u>, <u>you</u>, <u>her</u>, <u>him</u>, <u>us</u>, <u>them</u>.
Repeat the following examples after the speaker.

EXAMPLES	
I saw *him*.	They warned *you*.
They told *me*.	My dad helped *us*.
We asked *her*.	Put *them* on the table.

6. The demonstrative adjectives—<u>this</u>, <u>that</u>, <u>these</u>, and <u>those</u>—when followed by a noun.

Repeat the next examples after the speaker.

> EXAMPLES
>
> *This* book *is* interesting.
> *She* bought *that* house.
> *We* like *these* shoes.
> *Those* boys talk too loud.

7. Forms of the verb <u>be</u>—<u>am</u>, <u>are</u>, <u>is</u>, <u>was</u>, <u>were</u>, <u>aren't</u>, <u>isn't</u>, <u>wasn't</u>, <u>weren't</u>.

Say the following examples after the speaker.

EXAMPLES	
I *am* here.	We *were in the* garden.
He *is a* tall man.	He *wasn't* late.
They *are* all sick.	

8. The expressions <u>there is</u> and <u>there are</u>.
Repeat the examples after the speaker.

> EXAMPLES
>
> *There is a* car *in the* driveway.
> *There is* one apple *in the* basket.
> *There is* jewelry *in* that box.
> *There are* too many cars *on the* road.
> *There are* five people *in the* family.

9. The <u>to</u> before a verb.

Say the following examples after the speaker.

EXAMPLES

He needs *to* work.
I like *to* eat early.
M*y* mother loves *to* cook.
We want *to* see *the* whole movie.

---

10. Auxiliary verbs, such as <u>am</u>, <u>is</u>, <u>are</u>, <u>was</u>, <u>were</u>, <u>do</u>, <u>does</u>, <u>did</u>, <u>have</u>, <u>has</u>, <u>had</u>, <u>isn't</u>, <u>wasn't</u>, <u>didn't</u>, etc.

Listen to the following examples and repeat them after the speaker.

EXAMPLES

I *am* work*ing in the* house.
She *is* talk*ing on the* phone.
He *was* help*ing them*.
When *do* we start school?
Why *does* he travel so much?
Have you done *your* work?
We *have been* working all day.
He *had* always told *the* truth.
They *had* had *a* bad day.

---

11. Modal auxiliaries, such as <u>can</u>, <u>must</u>, <u>have to</u>, <u>should</u>, <u>could</u>, <u>would</u>, etc.

Repeat these examples after the speaker.

EXAMPLES

John *can* come.
Joe *has to* work.
Sam *should* leave.
We *would like to* help.
You *mustn't* go *in the* street.
Kathy *doesn't have to* work.

---

12. <u>Who</u>, <u>whose</u>, <u>when</u>, <u>where</u>, <u>why</u>, <u>what</u>, and <u>how</u> in the middle of a sentence.

Listen to these examples and repeat them after the speaker.

EXAMPLES

Jenny has *a* cousin *whose* name *is* Smith.
Do you know *where she* lives?
Only Courtney knows *why she* said that.
He didn't tell *me when to* come.
I can figure out *how to* do *it.*

---

13. Other short function words, such as <u>and</u>, <u>but</u>, <u>or</u>, <u>so</u>, <u>not</u>, <u>if</u>, <u>as</u>, <u>because</u>, <u>whether</u>, <u>since</u>, <u>until</u>, <u>though</u>, <u>although</u>.

Repeat the following examples after the speaker.

EXAMPLES

Mary *and* Bob have plenty *of* food, *such as* sandwiches, cakes, *and* cookies.
Joe, *not* John, *has been* here *since* noon.
Scott *was* worried *because his* wife *was so* late.
I'll stay *until he* calls, *then I'll* leave *so you can* study.
Although you're sick, *you can* eat *with* Carolyn *or* Sue.
I don't know *whether he was* late *or* not.
If you eat that much, *you'll be as* sick *as a* dog.

Exceptions

- The negative modal, <u>can't</u>, is usually stressed.
- When auxiliary verbs and modal auxiliaries are not followed by a verb, they have strong stress.

Listen to the following examples and repeat them after the speaker.

EXAMPLES

She can't help *him with the* cooking.
I'll come *to the* party *if I* can.
We would lend *you the* car *if we* could.
Carol has *a* new car, *but* Margaret doesn't.
He doesn't know *I'm* unhappy, *but I* am.

Practice for Mastery

Now practice the stress patterns discussed in this unit by repeating the following sentences after the speaker.

CD 4
TRACK 5

EXAMPLES

The money *is in the* bank.
He came over *to* talk *to me*.
She can help *him with the* cooking.
I should buy *a* new dress *for the* wedding.
We could lend *you our* car.
I will send *you a* letter tomorrow.
They're walking *to the* store.
He didn't work *because he was* sick.
Karen *and* Danny stayed *until they* knew
whether or not Val *was* coming.

- Any word can be given extra stress to emphasize or clarify a statement.

In the examples that follow, emphasis is shown in boldface. Listen, and repeat each sentence after the speaker.

	Meaning
I wanted to go to the **circus**.	(not the **movies**.)
They didn't go to **France**.	(They went to Paris, **Virginia**!)
I lost my ring on my way **to** the store.	(not **from** the store.)
He gave her the money.	(**I** didn't give her the money.)
He **gave** her the money.	(He didn't **lend** her the money.)
He gave **her** the money.	(He didn't give the money to **me**.)
He gave her the **money**.	(He didn't give her the **car**.)

Be careful not to use extra stress if you do not intend special meaning.

Next, listen to the following paragraph, paying close attention to the stress patterns.

> Learning to speak a language is a little like learning to dance. They both take a long time to master, but are fun from the beginning. Both require interaction with another person, who is saying or doing something different. Fluent speakers and good dancers don't have to think about their skills. They perform them naturally. To acquire these skills, you need a lot of practice and patience. Encouragement from someone else helps a great deal.

Now, repeat the paragraph, one phrase at a time, after the speaker.

Learning *to* speak
a language
is a little *like*
learning *to* dance.
They both take *a* long time
to master,
but are fun
from the beginning.
Both require interaction
with another person,
who is saying *or* doing
something different.
Fluent speakers
and good dancers
don't have to think
about their skills.
They perform *them* naturally.
To acquire *these* skills,
you need *a* lot *of* practice
and patience.
Encouragement *from* someone else
helps *a* great deal.

Read the paragraph aloud again, practicing the proper stress. Try recording your reading on tape to see if it sounds natural.

Here is another paragraph. Listen to it on your tape, noting the speaker's stress patterns.

Last May we had a surprise party at my house for one of my friends. It was his fiftieth birthday. We invited about thirty people, and most of them were able to come. One couple even traveled all the way from New Jersey. Several people who had been away for a long time were here. Most of the guests hadn't met each other before the party, but they were having a wonderful time talking during the half-hour before the birthday man arrived. It seemed that a very special person was a magnet for other special people. When he got here, he was really surprised, and happy to see so many friends. It was a good party.

Now, repeat each phrase after the speaker.

> Last May
> *we* had *a* surprise party
> *at my* house
> *for* one *of my* friends.
> *It was his* fiftieth birthday.
> *We* invited *about* thirty people,
> *and* most *of them*
> *were* able *to* come.
> One couple *even* traveled
> all *the* way *from* New Jersey.
> Several people
> *who had been* away
> *for a* long time
> *were* here.
> Most *of the* guests
> *hadn't* met each other
> *before the* party,
> *but they were* having
> *a* wonderful time talking
> *during the* half-hour
> *before the* birthday man arrived.
> *It* seemed
> *that a* very special person
> *was a* magnet
> *for* other special people.
> *When he* got here,
> *he was* really surprised,
> *and* happy *to* see
> *so* many friends.
> *It was a* good party.

Read the paragraph aloud again, comparing your stresses with those of the speaker.

PART FOUR
INTONATION
PATTERNS

Intonation is the "musical score" of a language. Each "tune" has a special meaning. In the following units, the intonation patterns are represented graphically: A horizontal line means that the words are all delivered at approximately the same pitch level; a rising line means that the pitch rises; a descending line means that it falls.

Unit Thirty-Eight
Greetings

Pattern ___ᐱ .

On your CD, listen to the intonation pattern in the following examples, and repeat them after the speaker.

EXAMPLES

Good morning.	Be careful.
Good afternoon.	Drive safely.
Good evening.	Say hello to your mother.
Good night.	Goodbye.
Hello.	Bye.
Hi.	Thank you.
Excuse me.	You're welcome.
Take care.	See you later.

When you say the name of the person you are talking to, add a second pattern to the previous greeting: __/ .

Now, repeat these phrases.

EXAMPLES

Good morning, Bill.
Good evening, Miss Jones.
Be careful, Emily.
Say hello to your mother, John.

Unit Thirty-Nine
Statements

Introducing the Patterns

Pattern 1: ___⋀ .

Listen to the speaker's intonation pattern in the following examples of one-phrase sentences, then repeat each sentence after the speaker.

> **EXAMPLES**
>
> She's my sister.   I have a dog.
> They're from Venezuela.   It's beautiful.
> We're going to visit them.   We love it.
> He's here.

Pattern 2: ___ʃ ___⋀ .

Listen to the following examples of two-phrase sentences, and repeat them after the speaker.

> **EXAMPLES**
>
> He's here, but she isn't.
> I have a dog, and you have a cat.
> She's my sister, and he's my cousin.
> When I see him, I'll tell him.
> After you get here, have a cup of coffee.
> Before you start, take a deep breath.

UNIT FORTY
QUESTIONS

Introducing the Patterns

Pattern 1: Tag Questions ___/\\ ___/ ?

This is the same pattern used for a greeting followed by a name. (See Unit Thirty-eight.)

Listen to and repeat each of the following sentences after the speaker.

> #### EXAMPLES
>
> He's coming, isn't he?
> You're a lawyer, aren't you?
> My sister told you, didn't she?
> You'll come to my party, won't you?

Pattern 2: Tag Questions Indicating Displeasure ___/\\ \~\\ ?

A message of displeasure can be conveyed through a different intonation pattern. Listen to the same sentences, noting the change in the speaker's tone and repeat each question after the speaker.

> #### EXAMPLES
>
> He's coming, isn't he?
> You're a lawyer, aren't you?
> My sister told you, didn't she?
> You'll come to my party, won't you?

This pattern can also indicate confidence in the response.

As before, repeat the example.

> **EXAMPLES**
>
> The water's nice, isn't it?

Pattern 3: Questions with Question Words ⌁?

You will note that this is the same pattern as that used in greetings and one-phrase statements. Try to imitate the speaker's tone.

Listen to and repeat each sentence after the speaker.

> **EXAMPLES**
>
> | | |
> |---|---|
> | When are you going? | Why are you crying? |
> | Who is the teacher? | Where did he go? |

When an answer to your question is suggested, it is on a higher tone: ⎯⎯⋀ ⎯⎯⟋

As before, repeat these examples after the speaker.

> **EXAMPLES**
>
> When are you going, Friday?
> Who is the teacher, Miss Smith?
> Why are you crying, to make me feel bad?
> Where did he go, to the movies?

The answers to the preceding questions have their own pattern: ⎯⎯⟍ . (pause) ⎯⎯⟍ .

Repeat these examples after the speaker.

> **EXAMPLES**
>
> | | |
> |---|---|
> | Yes. Friday. | No. I can't help it. |
> | No. Miss Jones. | Yes. To the movies. |

Pattern 4: Questions Indicating Annoyance ⌐\ ?

Next, repeat these questions that show annoyance through the intonation pattern.

EXAMPLES
Why do you ask? When is he coming? Where did you hear that? Who did this to you?

Pattern 5: Questions Without Question Words ___/ ?

Here is the last set of questions. As before, repeat each one after the speaker.

EXAMPLES	
Are you happy?	Was she there?
Will he win?	Were they hurt?
Do you like it?	Did you see it?

Introducing the Patterns

Fundamentally, the intonation pattern used in counting and listing is a series of level and rising tones that end with a final drop in pitch.

Counting

Listen to your CD and repeat the following examples after the speaker.

EXAMPLES

One, two, three, four, five.

Four hundred and thirty-seven, four hundred and thirty-eight, four hundred and thirty-nine, four hundred and forty.

Listing

As before, repeat these examples after the speaker.

EXAMPLES

I need shoes, socks, shirts, and pants.

He ate two hamburgers, french fries, and an ice cream cone.

She likes perfume, chocolates, flowers, and money.

Introducing the Patterns

Pattern 1: When the Question Requires a "Yes" or "No" Answer

Listen to your CD and repeat the questions after the speaker. Then listen for and repeat the answers.

EXAMPLES	
Question	**Answer**
Would you like potatoes or carrots?	No, I would rather have fruit.
Are you unhappy or uncomfortable?	No, I feel just fine.
Will he eat ice cream or cake?	Yes, he probably will (but he should be on a diet).
Would you like a drink or something?	Yes, please, I'm thirsty.

Pattern 2: When the Question Offers a Limited Choice

EXAMPLES	
Questions	**Answers**
Would you like potatoes or carrots?	I would like carrots.
Are you unhappy or uncomfortable?	I'm unhappy.
Will he eat ice cream or cake?	He'll have cake.

187

Practice in Context

Listen to the following dialogues on your CD and repeat each line after the speaker.

1. — Can you help me with these boxes, Steve?
   — No. I can't.
   — Why not?
   — They're too heavy. I hurt my back and I'm not sup-posed to lift anything heavy.
   — Well . . . how am I going to get them upstairs?
   — Call John and see if he'll help you!

2. — Hi, Carol. How are you?
   — Fine, thanks. How are you Ms. Johnson?
   — Fine. How's school these days?
   — Oh . . . it's O.K. but we have too much homework!
   — Are you going to the game?
   — Yes, are you?
   — No. I have to clean the garage.
   — O.K. . . . see you later.
   — Bye, drive carefully!

3. — Where are you going, Mom?
   — To the movies. Do you want to come?
   — Oh . . . I'd love to, but I have to go to the library.
   — The library! Wow! I'm really proud of you. Are you doing research?
   — No . . . I'm going to pick up my friends. They need a ride home.

4. — Come live with me in the city. You'll have lots of fun.
   — I don't like the city. It's too noisy. There's too much traffic and pollution, and there's no place to park. Why don't you come live with me in the country?
   — I hate the country. It's too far away, and there's more traffic out there than in the city. Besides, there's noth-ing to do there. Don't you get bored?
   — You're looking for an argument, aren't you? I can see we weren't meant for each other.
   — Don't be silly! I think this is a perfect relationship. I really like living alone.

APPENDIX

1. More Words to Practice

/ə/ in first syllable:	/ɪ/	/u/
*a*bout	did	bush
*a*bove	fig	cush*io*n
*a*dore	gin	pudding
*a*gain	his	cook
*a*head	kids	good
*a*jar	lip	hood
*a*llow	live	rook
*a*lone	pin	stood
*a*nnoy	sist*e*r	wool
*a*ppear	tin	wood
*a*round	win	would
*a*way	zip	should
*e*lect	building	
*e*merge	guild	
*e*nough	guilty	
*e*ssent*ia*l	quick	
*e*xact	quilt	
*e*xactly	cymb*a*l	
*o*bject	hymn	
*o*ccas*io*n	nymph	
*o*ffend		

CD 4
TRACK 13

/iy/	/uw/	/iuw/
	mood	pew
	boo hoo	hew
need	coo	Hugh
seed	goose	un*i*ty
deep	moon	un*iv*erse
keep	noon	un*iv*ersity
feel	soon	usef*u*l
creep	zoo	usu*a*l
squeeze	whose	util*i*ty
*e*xtreme	drew	fume
m*a*chine	grew	huge
squeal	Jew	munic*i*p*a*l
lead	jewel	mute
leap	jewelry	puny
please	stew	
tease	clue	
clean	glue	
floppy	true	
silly	juni*o*r	
lovely	truce	
friendly	tune	

CD 4 TRACK 14

/ʌ/	/ε/	/ow/
	beg	no
	bend	so
above	crept	loan
dove	leg	loaf
shove	lend	grown
ton	mend	shown
won	regret	known
bun	rest	stone
fun	send	phone
stuff	leapt	boulder
sun	pleasure	although
ugh	ready	dough
tough	stead	grow
	tread	blow
	jeopardy	show
		tow
		mow
		below
		Joe
		foe
		toe

/owr/	/oiy/	/eə/
bore	coin	
gore	Demoines	
more	groin	
store	join	
tore	loin	jam
dork	boy	can
fork	destroy	fan
forty	enjoy	land
north	joy	pan
short	ploy	ran
worn	soy	van
boor	toy	hand
floor		stand
poor		care
quart		dare
wart		fare
court		glare
your		pare
hoard		stare
roar		fair
		hair
		pair
		bear
		tear
		wear

CD 4
TRACK 15

/eiy/

CD 4
TRACK 16

crate	refrain
crave	remain
fate	stain
frame	train
grape	grey
lame	hey
late	prey
plane	whey
same	buffet
save	fillet
state	persuade
tame	feign
tape	freight
staple	neigh
clay	reign
fray	weigh
gray	weight
May	great
play	
pray	
stay	
cafe	
resumé	
gain	
grain	
plain	

/ɔ/

gone
belong
long
prong
song
wrong
call
fall
mall
tall
wall
auction
caucus
daunt
gaunt
haunted
jaundice
jaunt
jaunty
pause
raucous
taut
caught
fraught
haughty

/ɔ/ (cont'd.)	/ae/	
		CD 4 TRACK 17

/ɔ/ (cont'd.)	/ae/	/aəow/
taught	black	bower
bawdy	brat	brown
crawl	cap	clown
dawdle	castle	cow
flaw	crack	flower
jaw	dad	frown
lawn	dagger	howl
raw	dapper	jowl
saw	fasten	now
tawny	flag	owl
bought	flap	plow
brought	flat	prowl
fought	gag	shower
sought	gash	tower
thought	hash	town
wrought	hat	vowel
broad	jack	wow
	lack	dour
	lap	flour
	map	gouge
	nap	loud
	pack	mouse
	quack	mouth
	rack	our
	racquet	
	sack	
	sash	
	slash	
	stack	
	tack	
	trash	

/a/	/ar/	/aiy/
father	bar	bride
garage	barn	fire
ha ha	car	hire
Hawaii	carbs	I'm
wad	carve	I've
wash	dark	invite
watch	far	kind
yacht	farmer	quite
bother	farther	trite
clock	jar	twice
crop	lard	denied
flop	park	dried
mop	star	fried
office	starve	tie
plot	tar	tried
stock		blight
stop		flight
top		might
entree		plight
ennui		sigh
		slight
		haiku
		height
		cry
		cypress
		fry
		my
		buyer
		dye
		lye

CD 4
TRACK 18

CD 4
TRACK 19

2. Pronunciation differences when the letter e̲ is added to a one-syllable word

/I/	/aiy/	/aə/	/eiy/
bid	bide	bad	bade
hid	hide	mad	made
rid	ride	cam	came
Sid	side	dam	dame
dim	dime	gam	game
Tim	time	lam	lame
din	dine	Sam	same
fin	fine	sham	shame
pin	pine	tam	tame
win	wine	ban	bane
grip	gripe	can	cane
pip	pipe	Dan	Dane
rip	ripe	pan	pane
trip	tripe		

/ae/	/eiy/
fad	fade
lad	lade
gap	gape
rap	rape
cat	Cate
hat	hate
mat	mate
Nat	Nate
rat	rate